MARCEL DANESI

The Quest for Meaning

A Guide to Semiotic Theory and Practice

UNIVERSITY OF TORONTO PRESS
Toronto Buffalo London

© University of Toronto Press 2007
Toronto Buffalo London
Printed in Canada
Reprinted 2010, 2012

ISBN 978-0-8020-9368-4 (cloth)
ISBN 978-0-8020-9514-5 (paper)

Toronto Studies in Semiotics and Communication
Editors: Marcel Danesi, Umberto Eco, Paul Perron, Roland Posner,
Peter Schulz

Library and Archives Canada Cataloguing in Publication Data

Danesi, Marcel, 1946–
   The quest for meaning : a guide to semiotic theory and practice /
Marcel Danesi

(Toronto studies in semiotics and communication)
Includes index.
ISBN 978-0-8020-9368-4 (bound). – ISBN 978-0-8020-9514-5 (pbk.)

1. Semiotics – Textbooks.   I. Title.   II. Series.

P99.D285 2007   302.2   C2007-901542-5

The University of Toronto Press acknowledges the financial assistance to its
publishing program of the Canada Council for the Arts and the Ontario Arts
Council.

University of Toronto Press acknowledges the financial support for its
publishing activities of the Government of Canada through the
Book Publishing Industry Development Program (BPIDP).

Contents

THE QUEST FOR MEANING:
A GUIDE TO SEMIOTIC THEORY AND PRACTICE

Semiotics is the study of the most critical feature of human consciousness – the capacity to create and use signs such as words and symbols for thinking, communicating, reflecting, transmitting, and preserving knowledge. *The Quest for Meaning* is designed as a guide to basic semiotic theory and practice, discussing and illustrating the main trends, ideas, and figures of semiotics. Written as an introduction to the field, this study makes an otherwise complex discipline accessible to the interested reader.

Marcel Danesi examines the various themes, concepts, and techniques that constitute current semiotic theory, and does so in lucid, easy-to-follow language. Cross-references between topics show the interconnectedness of many aspects of semiotic practice and promote an understanding of the subject as a whole. Danesi treats such everyday things as food, clothing, mathematics, and popular culture to semiotic readings, providing basic examples of how the discipline can be applied in everyday life.

A step-by-step introduction, *The Quest for Meaning* is the definitive guide for students and teachers exploring semiotics at the undergraduate level and beyond.

(Toronto Studies in Semiotics and Communication)

MARCEL DANESI is a professor in the Department of Anthropology at the University of Toronto.

Preface

> The good of a book lies in its being read. A book is made up of signs that speak of other signs, which in their turn speak of things. Without an eye to read them, a book contains signs that produce no concepts; therefore it is dumb.
>
> Umberto Eco (b. 1932), *The Name of the Rose* (1983)

The 1983 English translation of semiotician Umberto Eco's *The Name of the Rose* turned that novel into an international best-seller. In 1985 a film based on the novel, directed by Jean-Jacques Annaud, became a box office hit. The unexpected success of the novel was due in part to the fact that it tapped into a late-twentieth-century resurgence of interest in legend, religion, mystery, and symbolism. The story is set in a cloistered medieval monastery in which monks are being murdered by a serial killer living among them. The monk who investigates the crimes is a learned Franciscan named William of Baskerville – a name that is transparently allusive of the fictional detective Sherlock Holmes and the dark and ominous setting found in Arthur Conan Doyle's classic detective story *The Hound of the Baskervilles* (1902). The monk solves the crimes in the manner and style of Sherlock Holmes, by detecting and interpreting the 'signs' left by the killer at each crime scene.

In 2003, Dan Brown's *The Da Vinci Code* became a runaway international best-seller and pop culture phenomenon; it was turned into a blockbuster movie in 2006. The hero, a Harvard scholar named Robert Langdon, solves an intriguing historical mystery connecting Jesus to Mary Magdalene by applying his knowledge of 'symbology.' Much of the allure of Brown's novel related to the hero's ability to interpret the signs of a mystery. Eco's novel and Brown's both became international bestsellers because – as those who study 'signs' know – the activity of unravelling mysteries by interpreting signs is how humans get to the bottom of things, both in fiction and in life. Human beings are interpreters of signs, and human history is essentially a testament to humanity's quest to understand the meanings of the signs that characterize human life. The study of this quest is called semiotics.

Semiotics is not just a technique that fictional detectives use to solve mysteries; it is an academic discipline in its own right that studies the most critical of all features of human sapience – the capacity to create and use signs (words, symbols, etc.) for thinking as well as for communicating and preserving knowledge. The formal study of signs is growing throughout the academic world, although it continues to struggle for mainstream acceptance. Yet it belongs in the mainstream alongside all other disciplines that aim to understand human sapience.

This book is meant to be a guide to basic semiotic theory and practice. However, I have not written it simply as an 'all you wanted to know about semiotics but were afraid to ask' book. The reader will need to make some effort to understand the subject matter of each of its seven chapters. Chapter 1 introduces the main trends, ideas, and figures in semiotics. Chapters 2 to 6 then deal with the topics that inform its theoretical apparatus and its methodology: signs, structure, codes, texts, and representation. Chapter 7 illustrates how semiotics can be applied productively to the study of material culture. The two specific areas I have chosen for illustration are clothing and food. Because the focus of this book is practical, I have kept references to the technical literature to a bare minimum and have used footnotes only when absolutely necessary.

To keep the proportions of this volume within the limits of a guidebook, I have had to restrict my choice of topics. All the same, I have tried to cast as wide a net as possible, so as to gather within two covers the main themes, concepts, and techniques that constitute current semiotic theory and practice. I advise the reader to supplement this treatment by consulting the works listed at the end of each chapter. It is my sincere hope that those who read this book will come away from it with a general idea of what semiotics is all about and why it is so important as an approach to gaining insight into our elusive and mysterious human nature.

Marcel Danesi
Program in Semiotics and Communication Theory
University of Toronto, 2007

THE QUEST FOR MEANING

1 What Is Semiotics?

Life has to be given a meaning because of the obvious fact that it has no meaning.

Henry Miller (1891–1980)

1.1 Introduction

Each time people experience excitement from reading a thriller, or shed tears while watching a sentimental movie, or chuckle at a cartoon strip, they are responding emotionally to the 'meanings' injected into these products by other human beings. Reading books, watching movies, and laughing at Homer Simpson are not exceptional activities or responses – they are behaviours that people in all walks of life engage in on a daily basis. Their ubiquity suggests that the need for meaning is as important as the procurement of biological survival. Perhaps they are even more important – news reports of people who willingly give up their lives for a 'cause' (read 'meaning') bear this out rather dramatically.

It can be argued that the need for 'produced meanings' constitutes a small-scale version of humanity's larger-scale need to unravel the 'meaning of life.' Studying the latter has always been the project of philosophy and theology as well as various other disciplines; studying the former is the specific task of semiotics, which we can define simply as the 'science of produced meaning.' The ultimate goal of semiotics is, in fact, to unravel the meanings that are built into all kinds of human products, from words, symbols, narratives, symphonies, paintings, and comic books to scientific theories and mathematical theorems. At first glance, this task might seem daunting, as it encompasses virtually all the creative and knowledge-making activities that make up human social life. But it is not, because semiotics focuses more narrowly on the use, structure, and function of the signs (symbols, words, images, figures, etc.) used in these activities. Ultimately, though, it produces insights that relate to the larger question of the meaning of existence.

Consider, as an initial example of semiotic analysis, the sign formed by raising the index and middle fingers in the shape of a V.

If asked what it means, most people today would answer that it stands for 'victory' or 'peace.' Why is this so? After all, two fingers are two fingers. What possible connection could they have to victory or peace? As it turns out, the sign's link to victory spread through contemporary society at the end of the Second World War, after British politician Winston Churchill (1874–1965) utilized it publicly to underscore the Allied victory. Churchill evidently formed the sign to resemble the first letter of the English word 'victory.' A generation later, the same sign underwent a drastic transformation in meaning, aided by the popularity of the *Star Trek* series on network television, where it surfaced as the Vulcan peace sign, signifying 'Live long and prosper.' The Vulcan sign was formed with the third and fourth fingers instead of the second and third (see the next page). This 'peace meaning' of the V-sign caught on quickly in the emerging counterculture of the late 1960s. Indeed, the hippies used it deliberately as a symbol to warn society of the inanity of war and human conflict.

But the semiotic story of the V-sign (however it is made) does not stop here. It can also be used much more practically to indicate the number '2' or the letter 'V' itself. Moreover, in some cultures it is used as a greeting sign, while in others it stands for 'femininity' and 'fertil-

ity.' Now, explaining meanings associated with the V-sign such as '2' or 'victory' is a fairly simple task. On the other hand, explicating a meaning such as 'femininity' is not. Here, the semiotician becomes a 'detective' and, like a true detective, must start by considering the shape of the sign itself as an initial clue for unravelling the reasons underlying the meaning. The V-shape seems to suggest the physiognomy of female sexuality as a receptacle or a vessel, in much the same way that phallic symbols suggest male sexuality – namely, through resemblance. Of course, in this particular case the semiotician can only raise this possibility, and look for corroborating evidence among the symbolic and representational traditions of cultures around the world that use the V-sign with this meaning, as well as in current manifestations. A contemporary version of this sign can, by the way, be observed in its use to indicate 'girl power' – a use that, to the best of my knowledge, was brought into the pop culture domain in the mid-1990s by a British rock group called the Spice Girls.

The above discussion encapsulates what semiotics is essentially all about. Its central aim is to investigate, decipher, document, and explain the *what*, *how*, and *why* of signs, no matter how simple or complex they are. Since the middle part of the twentieth century, semiotics has grown into a broad field of inquiry. It has been applied to the study of body language, art forms, discourses of all kinds, visual communication, media, advertising, narratives, language, objects, gestures, facial expressions, eye contact, clothing, space, cuisine, rituals – in sum, to everything that human beings produce and use to communicate and represent things in some psychologically and socially meaningful way. But this seemingly eclectic pastiche of applications is hardly random or haphazard. It has a specific purpose – to flesh out recurrent patterns in the production of human meaning.

1.2 A Historical Sketch

The historical sketch that follows makes no pretensions to being exhaustive. It is intended simply to provide major points of reference for discussing semiotic concepts and practices in this and later chapters.

The term *semeiotics* (now spelled without the 'e') – from the Greek *sêmeiotikos*, 'observant of signs' – was coined by Hippocrates (c. 460–c. 370 BCE), the founder of Western medicine, to designate the study of the warning signs produced by the human body, referred to more commonly today as symptoms. Hippocrates argued that the particular physical form that a symptom takes – called a *semeion* ('mark') – constitutes a vital clue to its source. Its visible features 'announce,' so to speak, that 'something invisible' – a disease, malady, or ailment – is present in the body. With this simple concept, Hippocrates established medicine as a diagnostic 'semeiotic' science – that is, a science based on the detection and interpretation of bodily signs. Semeiotic method was entrenched permanently in medical practice shortly afterwards by the physician Galen of Pergamum (c. 130–c. 200 CE).

The concept of *semeion* as 'something physical' standing for 'something else' was expanded in antiquity to include human-made semeions (such as words) that stood for psychological or emotional states. Among the first to differentiate between physical and human-made or conventional semeions was the Greek philosopher Plato (c. 427–c. 347 BCE). Plato was intrigued by the fact that a single word has the capacity to refer not only to specific objects, but also to objects that resemble one another in some identifiable way. For example, the word *circle* does not refer to a singular thing (although it can if need be), but rather to anything that has the property 'circularity' – a particular circle can be altered in size, but it will still be called a *circle* because it possesses this property. Plato concluded that the ideas we encode with words can't possibly be part of our everyday world, which is changing and imperfect. They possess, he suggested, inherent properties that mirror innate forms in the mind. It is these properties that are captured by words.

As Plato realized, words reveal something remarkable about human understanding – namely, our propensity to unravel the essence of things, not just name and classify them as individual objects. In any case, the latter would be impossible because there would then be as many words as there are things. Plato's pupil Aristotle (384–322 BCE)

took issue with this particular aspect of his teacher's philos
arguing that words start out not as properties but rather as practical
strategies for naming singular things. Only after we discover that
certain things have similar properties do we start classifying them into
categories. At such points of discovery, Aristotle argued, we create
abstract words that allow us to bring together things that have similar
properties: plants, animals, objects, and so on. In contrast to Plato's
'mentalist' theory, Aristotle's theory is referred to as 'empirical.' Both
theories make sense, and neither can be proved or disproved. To this
day, the debate between mentalists and empiricists rages on, indicating that it will probably never be resolved.

Eventually, a question arose: Is there any connection between
natural and conventional signs? Among the first to discuss a possible
relationship between the two were the Stoics. Stoicism was a Greek
school of philosophy that emerged around 308 BCE. The Stoics argued
that conventional signs (words and symbols) reveal something intrinsic about the nature of human psychological and emotional states in
the same way that natural signs reveal something intrinsic about biological states. Is this a tenable view? Are natural and conventional
signs – for example, symptoms and words – linked in some way?
Semioticians have always debated this question. St Augustine
(354–430 CE), the early church father and philosopher, was among the
first to argue for a fundamental difference between the two in his *De
doctrina christiana* (On Christian Doctrine). He posited that natural
signs *(signa naturalia)* are distinct from conventional ones because they
are products of nature and thus lack intentionality. Such signs include
not only bodily symptoms but also the rustling of leaves, the colours
of plants, the signals that animals emit, and so on. Conventional signs
(signa data), on the other hand, are the product of human intentions.
These include not only words but also gestures and the many symbols
that humans have invented to serve their psychological, social, and
communicative needs. Finally, St Augustine considered miracles to be
messages from God and thus sacred signs. These can only be understood on faith, although such understanding is based in part on specific cultural interpretations of them.

Interest in linking human understanding with sign production
waned after St Augustine's death. Only in the eleventh century was
interest rekindled, mainly through the translation of the works of
Plato, Aristotle, and other important Greek philosophers. The
outcome was the movement known as Scholasticism. The Scholastics

were Christian thinkers whose aim was to solve long-standing theological problems, such as the provability of God's existence. Using Aristotelian empiricist theory as their basic modus operandi, they asserted that conventional signs capture practical truths and do not construct them out of mere convenience. However, within this movement there were some – referred to as nominalists – who argued that 'truth' is itself a matter of subjective opinion and that at best, signs capture illusory and highly variable human versions of truth. For instance, John Duns Scotus (c. 1266–1308) and William of Ockham (c. 1285–c. 1349) stressed that signs end up referring to other signs rather than to actual things or Platonic properties – a perspective that is strikingly similar to some modern theories of the sign, as we shall see in due course. The theologian St Thomas Aquinas (1225–74) countered with the idea that signs do indeed refer to real things and categories of things, even if they constitute variable human models of them. At about the same time, the English philosopher and scientist Roger Bacon (c. 1214–c. 1292) developed one of the first comprehensive typologies of signs, contending that without a firm understanding of the role of signs in human understanding, discussing what truth is or is not can only end up being a trivial matter of subjective opinion.

Two centuries later, after the Polish astronomer Copernicus (1473–1543) arrived at the theory of heliocentricity (i.e., the earth orbits the sun), a powerful new intellectual movement took shape in Western society. This movement placed science ahead of religion and philosophy as the primary form of inquiry for grasping truths about reality. This movement was spearheaded by the scientists themselves, especially Francis Bacon (1561–1626) and Galileo Galilei (1564–1642). A little later, philosophers joined the scientists, contending that all forms of reality, physical and psychological, can be studied in ways that parallel the scientific approach – a view scattered throughout the writings of Thomas Hobbes (1588–1679), René Descartes (1596–1650), Benedict Spinoza (1632–77), Gottfried Wilhelm Leibniz (1646–1716), David Hume (1711–76), and John Locke (1632–1704). Needless to say, there were some who went against this intellectual grain. For instance, the Irish prelate George Berkeley (1685–1753) detested science and mathematics, arguing that they were nothing but fanciful concoctions of the human mind; and the German philosopher Immanuel Kant (1724–1804) suggested, in an analogous fashion, that any scientific claim to truth can only be an illusory one because science is itself a product of human fancy. Kant's ideas laid the groundwork for the Romantic movement in philosophy and the arts – a movement manifested especially in the writings of Friedrich Nietzsche (1844–1900), Edmund Husserl (1859–1938), and, later, Martin Heidegger (1889–1976) – which claimed that true knowledge of the world is an unattainable ideal.

A particularly important figure in the development of sign theory in the post-Copernican era was John Poinsot (1589–1644), who in *Treatise on Signs* (1632) defined the sign as an intermediary between thoughts and things. Poinsot suggested that signs function psychologically as 'intermediary forms' that allow the human mind to make a direct link to the 'realities' of life. These realities can thus be studied in the actual forms we make. A half century later, Locke suggested a specific plan for incorporating the formal study of signs into philosophy in his *Essay Concerning Human Understanding* (1690). Locke saw semiotics as an investigative instrument for philosophers, rather than a distinct discipline or method of inquiry. The idea of fashioning an autonomous discipline of sign study did not crystallize until the late nineteenth century, when the Swiss linguist Ferdinand de Saussure (1857–1913) proposed this in *Cours de linguistique générale* (1916), a textbook compiled after his death by two of his university students. Saussure used the term *sémiologie* (English *semiology*) – which he had used in personal correspondence as far back as 1894 – to designate the new discipline.

As the following extract from the *Cours* shows, Saussure suggested that the main goal of semiology (should it ever come into being) would be to understand the social function of signs:[1]

> It is possible to conceive of a science which studies the role of signs as part of social life. It would form part of social psychology, and hence of general psychology. We shall call it *semiology* (from the Greek *semeion*, 'sign'). It would investigate the nature of signs and the laws governing them. Since it does not yet exist, one cannot say for certain that it will exist. But it has a right to exist, a place ready for it in advance. Linguistics is only one branch of this general science. The laws which semiology will discover will be laws applicable in linguistics, and linguistics will thus be assigned to a clearly defined place in the field of human knowledge.

Saussure went on to suggest that of all sign systems, language is 'the most complex and universal,'[2] and that this is so because 'There are no pre-existing ideas, and nothing is distinct before the appearance of language.'[3]

Saussure seems to have been unaware that the French term *sémiologie* first appeared, so it seems, in *Dictionnaire de Trévoux* (1752), where it had a medical meaning. Also, the *Imperial Dictionary*, published in England in 1883, included an entry for *semeiology*, defining it as the 'doctrine of signs.' Today, Locke's term *(semeiotics)*, spelled *semiotics*, is the preferred one, having been adopted by the International Association of Semiotic Studies in 1969. The term *significs*, coined by Victoria Lady Welby (1837–1912) in 1896, is also used occasionally in the technical literature, but with a specific sense – the study of the relations among signs and the emotions. It was the American philosopher Charles S. Peirce (1839–1914) who brought Locke's term into wide circulation. Along with Saussure, Peirce is the founder of modern semiotics. Peirce's writing style is rather dense and his ideas are not easily grasped; even so, his basic theory of the sign has become a key one. Perhaps his greatest insight is that our sensory and emotional experience of the world influences how a sign is constituted and why it has been brought into existence in the first place. We construct a semeion not because we simply want to refer to something in particular or classify it as part of some category, but because we wish to understand that something in a sensory-based way. This can be heard clearly in imitative or onomatopoeic words such as *buzz* and *murmur*, which are designed to resemble the sounds associated with the objects or actions to which they refer. But the very same modelling process occurs across meaning systems, as we shall see in due course.

Following Saussure and Peirce, a number of people developed semiotics into the sophisticated discipline that it is today. Only a few will be mentioned in passing here. Ludwig Wittgenstein (1889–1951) suggested that signs are pictures of reality, presenting it as if it were a series of frames. This 'picture view' continues to inform a large part of semiotic theory and practice. The American semiotician Charles Morris (1901–79) subdivided semiotic method as follows: the study of sign assemblages, which he called *syntactics*; the analysis of the relations that are forged between signs and their meanings, which he called *semantics*; and the investigation of the relations that are formed between signs and their users, which he called *pragmatics*. The Russian-born American semiotician Roman Jakobson (1896–1982) studied various facets of sign construction but is probably best known for his model of communication, which suggests that sign exchanges are hardly ever neutral, but involve subjectivity and goal attainment of some kind. The French semiotician Roland Barthes (1915–80) illustrated the power of semiotics for decoding the hidden meanings in pop culture spectacles such as wrestling matches and Hollywood blockbusters. Another French semiotician, Algirdas J. Greimas (1917–92), developed the branch of semiotics known as *narratology*, which studies how human beings in different cultures invent similar kinds of narratives (myths, tales, etc.) with virtually the same stock of characters, motifs, themes, and plots. The Hungarian-born American semiotician Thomas A. Sebeok (1920–2001) was influential in expanding the semiotic paradigm to include the comparative study of animal signalling systems, which he termed *zoosemiotics*, and the study of semiosis in all living things, which has come to be called *biosemiotics*. Semiosis is the innate ability to produce and comprehend signs in a species-specific way. Sebeok contended that the interweaving and blending of ideas, findings, and discourses from different disciplinary domains is the distinguishing feature of biosemiotics. Finally, the Italian semiotician Umberto Eco (b. 1932) has contributed significantly to our understanding of how we interpret signs. It was Eco who single-handedly put semiotics on the map of pop culture with his best-selling novel *The Name of the Rose*.

Readers are also bound to come across names such as Derrida, Lévi-Strauss, Merleau-Ponty, Deleuze, Ricoeur, Deely, Merrell, Lotman, Hjelmslev, Kristeva, Lacan, Foucault, Lady Welby, Bénveniste, and Langer, among others, when reading about signs and sign theory in various sources. Some of these people will be mentioned later in this book. Because of space limitations many others will not be, even though their influence on semiotic theory and practice has hardly been negligible. The monumental treatise on the development of sign theory by John Deely is recommended as a resource for filling in the gaps left here.[4]

1.3 The Science of Meaning

As already noted, semiotics can be defined simply as the science of meaning. But how does one go about scientifically studying something as elusive as meaning, since unlike physical objects, it cannot be handled or described separately from the products that are constructed to contain it (words, symbols, etc.)? In fact, there *is* a way to do so rather easily – namely, by studying those very products in order to determine how they convey meaning and then reconstructing the various forms of meaning by inference. Instead of studying meaning by contemplating it directly, as traditional philosophy does, semiotics studies how it is built into signs and texts of all kinds (words, symbols, drawings, musical compositions, etc.). In short, semiotics studies 'produced meaning' in order to understand semiosis. Semiotics is often confused with communication science. Although the two fields share much of the same theoretical and methodological territory, the latter focuses more on the technical study of how messages are transmitted (vocally, electronically, etc.) and on the mathematical and psychological laws governing the transmission, reception, and processing of information. Semiotics, by contrast, pays more attention to *what* information is and *how* we interpret it.

What is *meaning*? A little reflection tells us that this is a confusing word indeed. As the literary critics C.K. Ogden and I.A. Richards showed in their masterful 1923 work *The Meaning of Meaning*, there are at least twenty-three definitions of the word *meaning* in English, which of course adds to the confusion.[5] Here are some of them:

Alex *means* to watch that show.	=	'intends'
A red light *means* stop.	=	'indicates'
Happiness *means* everything.	=	'has importance'
Sarah's look was full of *meaning*.	=	'special import'
Does life have a *meaning*?	=	'purpose'
What does love *mean* to you?	=	'convey'

To avoid such ambivalence, the terms *reference, sense,* and *definition* are often used instead of *meaning* in both philosophy and semiotics. Reference is the process of pointing out or identifying something; sense is what that something elicits psychologically, historically, and socially; and definition is a statement about what that something means by convention. Words can refer to the same (or similar) things, known as *referents*, yet have different *senses*. For example, the 'long-eared, short-tailed, burrowing mammal of the family Leporidae' can be called *rabbit* or *hare* in English. Both words *refer* essentially to the same kind of mammal. But there is a difference of sense between the two – *hare* is the more appropriate term for describing the mammal if it is larger, has longer ears and legs, and does not burrow. Another difference is that a *rabbit* is now viewed as a 'pet,' whereas a *hare* is unlikely to be viewed as such. The German philosopher Gottlob Frege (1848–1925) was among the first to point out the importance of sense phenomena in theories of meaning. Frege's now classic example was that of the 'fourth smallest planet and the second planet from the Sun' as being named both *Venus* and the *Morning Star*. The two terms refer to the same thing, he observed, but they have different senses: *Venus* designates the planet in a straightforward referential way (nevertheless with implicit references to the goddess of sexual love and physical beauty of Roman mythology), whereas *Morning Star* brings out the fact that the planet is visible in the east just before sunrise. Knowledge of signs, as this example shows, includes awareness of the senses that they bear in social and historical context – a fact emphasized further by the philosopher Willard V.O. Quine (1908–2000). In what has become a classic example in modern-day philosophy of the inherent difference between referential and sense-based meaning, Quine portrayed a situation in which a linguist overhears *Gavagai* from the mouth of a native informant when a rabbit is sighted scurrying through the bushes. But the linguist cannot determine whether the word means 'rabbit,' 'undetached rabbit parts,' or 'rabbit stage' because, as he has discovered from the informants, these are all senses that the word evokes. The meaning, therefore, will remain indeterminate unless it can be inferred from the context in which *Gavagai* occurs.

Definition, as mentioned, is a statement about what something means put together by using words and other signs (e.g., pictures). As useful as it is, the act of defining something such as a word leads inevitably to circularity. Take the dictionary definition of *cat*: 'a small carnivorous mammal domesticated since early times as a catcher of rats and mice and as a pet and existing in several distinctive breeds and varieties.' One of the problems that immediately surfaces from this definition relates to the use of *mammal* to define *cat*. In effect, one term has been replaced by another. So, what is the meaning of *mammal*? A *mammal*, the dictionary states, is 'any of various warm-blooded vertebrate animals of the class Mammalia.' But this definition is hardly a viable way out of the growing circle of references. What is an *animal*? The dictionary defines *animal* as an *organism*, which it defines, in turn, as an individual form of *life*, which it then defines as the property that distinguishes living *organisms*. Alas, at that point the dictionary has gone into a referential loop, since it has employed an already used concept, *organism*, to define *life*. This looping pattern surfaces in all domains of human knowledge. It suggests that signs can never be understood in the absolute, only in relation to other signs.

In contemporary semiotics the terms *denotation* and *connotation* are preferred to reference and sense. Consider, again, the word *cat*. The word elicits an image of a 'creature with four legs, whiskers, retractile claws,' and so on. This is its *denotative* meaning, which is intended to point out what distinguishes a *cat* – a mammal with 'retractile claws,' 'long tail,' and so on – from some other mammal. This allows us to determine whether something real or imaginary under consideration is an exemplar of a 'cat.' Similarly, the word *square* refers to a figure characterized by the distinctive features 'four equal straight lines' and 'meeting at right angles.' It is irrelevant whether the lines are thick, dotted, 2 metres long, 80 feet long, or coloured differently. If the figure has 'four equal straight lines meeting at right angles,' it qualifies as a square. The word *denotation*, incidentally, is derived from the compound Latin verb *de noto*, 'to mark out, point out, specify, indicate.' The noun *nota* ('mark, sign, note') itself derives from the verb *nosco* ('to come to know,' 'to become acquainted with,' 'to recognize').

All other senses associated with the words *cat* and *square* are connotative – that is, they are derivational or extensional. Some connotative senses of *square* can be seen in expressions such as the following:

She's so *square*.	=	'old fashioned'
He has a *square* disposition.	=	'forthright,' 'honourable'
Put it *squarely* on the table.	=	'evenly,' 'precisely'

Notice that an old-fashioned person, an honourable individual, and the action of laying something down nevertheless imply the referential meaning of 'square.' The concept of 'square' is an ancient one and thus probably known by everyone (hence 'old-fashioned'); it is also a figure with every part equal (hence 'forthright'); and it certainly is an even-sided figure (hence 'evenly'). Connotation encompasses all kinds of senses, including emotional ones. Consider the word *yes*. Besides being a sign of affirmation, it can have various emotional senses depending on the tone of voice with which it is uttered. When one says it with a raised tone – as in a question, 'Yes?' – then it conveys doubt or incredulity. When articulated emphatically – 'Yes!' – then it connotes triumph, achievement, or victory.

Connotation is the operative sense-making and sense-extracting mode in the production and decipherment of creative texts such as poems, novels, musical compositions, works of art – in effect, of most of the non-technical texts that people create. But this does not imply that meaning in technical (information-based) domains is exclusively denotative. On the contrary, many (if not all) scientific theories and models involve connotative processes, even though they end up being interpreted denotatively over time. This topic will be examined more closely in subsequent chapters. Above all else, it should be emphasized that connotation is not an option, as some traditional theories of meaning continue to sustain to this day; rather, it is something we are inclined to extract from a sign. The V-sign discussed above (§1.1), for example, has a denotative meaning, as we saw – it can be used to represent the number 2 – but only in response to a question such as, 'How many dollars do you have in your pocket?' This denotative meaning – two fingers representing the number 2 directly – is established by a very limitative context. In all other contexts the V-sign elicits connotative interpretations. This applies to all kinds of signs – even to digits. The numbers 7 and 13 in our culture invariably reverberate with connotative meanings such as 'fortune,' 'destiny,' 'bad luck,' and so on. By the way, such meanings are hardly fanciful or dismissible. They tend to have real-world consequences, notwithstanding their apparent superstitious senses. This can be seen, for instance, in the fact that many high-rise buildings in our society do not label the 'thirteenth floor' as such, but rather as the 'fourteenth,' in order to avoid the possibility of inviting the bad fortune associated connotatively with the number 13 to the building and its residents.

Abstract concepts such as 'motherhood,' 'masculinity,' 'friendship,' and 'justice' are especiallly high in connotative content. In 1957 the psychologists Osgood, Suci, and Tannenbaum showed this empirically by applying a technique called the *semantic differential*, which is designed to flesh out the connotative (culture-specific) meanings that abstract concepts elicit.[6] It consists in posing a series of questions to subjects about a particular concept – *Is X good or bad? Should Y be weak or strong?* and so on. The subjects are asked to rate the concept on seven-point scales. The ratings are then collected and analysed statistically in order to sift out any general patterns.

Suppose that subjects are asked to rate the concept 'ideal American president' in terms of the following scales: for example, *Should the pres-*

ident be young or old? Should the president be practical or idealistic? Should the president be modern or traditional? and so on:

| young | _ _ _ _ _ _ _ | old |
| | 1 2 3 4 5 6 7 | |

| practical | _ _ _ _ _ _ _ | idealistic |
| | 1 2 3 4 5 6 7 | |

| modern | _ _ _ _ _ _ _ | traditional |
| | 1 2 3 4 5 6 7 | |

| attractive | _ _ _ _ _ _ _ | bland |
| | 1 2 3 4 5 6 7 | |

| friendly | _ _ _ _ _ _ _ | stern |
| | 1 2 3 4 5 6 7 | |

A subject who feels that the president should be more 'youngish' than 'oldish' would place a mark towards the *young* end of the top scale; one who feels that a president should be 'bland' would place a mark towards the *bland* end of the *attractive–bland* scale; and so on. If we were to ask a large number of subjects to rate the president in this way, we would get a 'connotative profile' of the American presidency in terms of the statistically significant variations in sense that it evokes. Interestingly, research utilizing the semantic differential has shown that the range of variations is not a matter of pure subjectivity, but forms, rather, a socially based pattern. In other words, the connotations of many (if not all) abstract concepts are constrained by culture. For example, the word *noise* turns out to be a highly emotional concept for the Japanese, who rate it consistently at the ends of the scales presented to them; whereas it is a fairly neutral concept for Americans, who tend to rate it on average in the mid-ranges of the same scales. Connotation is not, therefore, open-ended; it is constrained by a series of factors, including conventional agreements as to what signs mean in certain situations. Without such constraints, our systems of meaning, known as *signification* systems, would be virtually unusable. All signification (be it denotative or connotative) is a relational and associative process – that is, signs acquire their meanings not in isolation, but in relation to other signs and to the contexts in which they occur.

As mentioned, the distinction between denotation and connotation is by and large analogous to Frege's distinction between reference and sense. And indeed, these terms are used interchangeably in the relevant semiotic literature, as are Rudolf Carnap's (1891–1970) terms *intension* (= denotation) and *extension* (= connotation). While there are subtle differences among these terms, it is beyond the present purpose to compare them. Suffice it to say that in current semiotic practice they are virtually synonymous:

reference	=	denotation	=	intension
sense	=	connotation	=	extension

The use of the denotation vs connotation dichotomy is often credited to philosopher John Stuart Mill (1806–73); in actual fact, though, it can be traced back to the medieval Scholastics, and in particular to William of Ockham (§1.2). In both Ockham and Mill, however, connotation is used to indicate the sum of the properties that a word's referent is perceived to have. The distinction between denotation and connotation as we understand it today was made for the first time by the American linguist Leonard Bloomfield in his influential 1933 book *Language*.[7] The same distinction was fleshed out later by the Danish linguist Louis Hjelmslev (1899–1965); Hjelmslev's treatment is highly abstruse and largely confusing; even so, it has placed this basic distinction on the semiotic agenda once and for all. Especially relevant is Hjelmslev's characterization of connotation as a 'secondary semiotic system' for expressing subjective meanings. Barthes and Greimas (§1.2) later argued that connotation is an inbuilt feature of signs, not just a matter of individual choice.

At this point it is important to distinguish between the terms *image* and *concept*, which are also used interchangeably in the semiotic literature even though there is a difference. The former is the mental picture of a referent that is evoked when a sign is used or suggested; the latter is the culture-specific interpretation that is assigned to that picture. There are two types of concept: concrete and abstract. The former is any referent that can be seen, heard, smelled, touched, or tasted – that is, observed in some direct sensory way; the latter is any referent that cannot be perceived in a direct sensory fashion. A 'cat' constitutes a concrete concept because a real cat can be observed with the senses. On the other hand, 'love' is an abstract concept because, although it can be experienced emotionally, it cannot be observed directly – that is, the emotion itself cannot be separated from the behaviours, states of mind, and so on that it produces.

The distinction between concrete and abstract concepts is a general one. In actual fact, there are many degrees or levels of concreteness and abstraction, which are influenced by social, historical, and other kinds of external or contextual factors. Generally, semioticians and psychologists posit the existence of three such levels. At the highest, referred to as the *superordinate* level, concepts are considered to have a highly general classificatory (abstract) function. So, for example, in the dictionary definition of *cat*, the related concept of *mammal* would be viewed as a superordinate concept because it refers to the general category of animals to which a cat belongs. Then there is the *basic* or *prototypical* level, which is where the word *cat* itself would fit in. This is the level where basic types of mammals are classified – cats, dogs, goats, hogs, horses, and the like. The third level, called the *subordinate* level, is where more detailed ways of referring to something occur. There are in fact many types (breeds) of cat – Siamese, Persian, Abyssinian, Korat, and so forth – which allow us to refer to differences in detail perceived as relevant. However, such notions as levels and hierarchies are problematic, as Umberto Eco pointed out in *Semiotics and the Philosophy of Language* (1984).[8] The main difficulty, he suggested, is that decisions as to where a concept belongs in a hierarchy invariably end up being a matter of subjective choice. Rather than hierarchical structure, Eco and other semioticians suggest that they have associative structure (see §3.3).

Ultimately, signs allow people to recognize certain patterns in the world over and over again; in this way they serve as directive guides for taking action in the world. Signs are thus closely tied to social needs and aspirations – a fact emphasized by many semioticians, especially the Russian theorist Mikhail Bakhtin (1895–1975). Bakhtin went so far as to argue that signs gain meaning only as they are exchanged by people in social dialogue or discourse. In effect, he maintained that all human meaning is constructed dialogically (socially). In my view, this is only partially correct. Some caution must be exercised in adopting social theories of meaning à la Bakhtin. The fact is that there is a constant interaction between nature and culture, or between the *biosphere* and the *semiosphere*, in the production of signs, as the great biologist Jakob von Uexküll (1864–1944) and the Estonian cultural semiotician Jurij Lotman (1922–93) argued. It is more accurate to say that concept formation is the result of adaptation partly to the biosphere and partly to the semiosphere – that is, to the universe of signs in which humans are reared. The notion of semiosphere will be taken up in §4.5. Suffice it to say here that it seems to resolve the controversy between 'constructivists' like Bakhtin and those who contend that everything we know is hard-wired in the brain at birth ('universalists').

1.4 Two Fundamental Models of the Sign

The elemental question that motivates semiotic inquiry is this: How does semiosis occur? Answers to this question are guided today by two fundamental models of the sign – the one put forward by Saussure and the one elaborated by Peirce.

Saussure was born in Geneva in 1857. He attended science classes at the University of Geneva before turning to language studies at the University of Leipzig in 1876. In 1879, while still a student, he published his only book, *Mémoire sur le système primitif des voyelles dans les langues indo-européennes* (Memoir on the Original Vowel System in the Indo-European Languages), an important work on the vowel system of Proto-Indo-European, considered the parent language from which the Indo-European languages have descended. Saussure taught at the École des Hautes Études in Paris from 1881 to 1891 and then became a professor of Sanskrit and comparative grammar at the University of Geneva. He never wrote another book; however, his teaching proved to be highly influential. After his death, two of his students compiled the lecture notes they had taken in his classes, as well as other materials related to the course, and wrote the seminal work *Cours de linguistique générale* (1916), which bears Saussure's name.

Saussure suggested, first and foremost, that any true semiological science should include *synchronic* and *diachronic* components. The former involves studying sign systems at a given point in time – normally the present – and the latter how they change over time. As a simple case in point of what diachronic analysis involves, consider the word *person*, which derives from the Latin word *persona*, meaning a 'mask' worn by an actor on stage. The Romans probably adopted it from an even earlier Etruscan word, *phersu*, perhaps by way of Greek. Subsequently, it came to have the meaning 'the character of the mask wearer' on the stage. That meaning exists to this day in the theatre term *dramatis personae*, 'cast of characters' (more literally 'the persons of the drama'). Eventually the word came to have its present meaning of 'human being' – an outcome that brings out the influence that the theatre has had in human society. This analysis of *person* also provides insight into why we continue to this day to use theatrical expressions such as *to play a role in life, to interact, to act out feelings, to put on a proper face* (mask), and so on to describe the activities and behaviours of 'persons.' The theatre itself may in fact have come about in order to make life intelligible. With its characters and plots, it continues to have great emotional power because it puts *life* on display in a concrete and understandable way. The linkage between personality and the theatre is also the reason why we commonly resort to theatre terms in conversations about people and their lives. For example, if we ask someone 'What is your life like?' we often get responses such as 'My life is a comedy' or 'My life is a farce,' from which we can draw specific inferences about the person's life.

Saussure put forward a 'binary' model of the sign – a structure with two components, physical and conceptual. He termed the physical part of the sign, such as the sounds that make up the word *cat*, the *signifier*, and the concept that the sign elicits, the *signified* (literally, 'that which is signified by the sign'). Saussure contended, moreover, that there is no necessary motivation or reason for creating the word *cat* other than the social need to do so. Any other signifier would have done the job just as effectively. This is why his model of the sign is called 'arbitrary.' This topic will be revisited in due course.

Peirce was born in Cambridge, Massachusetts, in 1839. He was educated at Harvard University. He lectured on logic and philosophy at Johns Hopkins and Harvard, where he expanded the system of logic created by the British mathematician George Boole (1815–64). But Peirce is best known for his view, called *pragmatism*, which maintains that the significance of any theory or model lies in the practical effects of its application. Pragmatism was incorporated by William James (1842–1910) into psychology and by John Dewey (1859–1952) into education, profoundly influencing modern-day practices in those two fields. In contrast to the Saussurean model of the sign, the Peircean model is referred to as 'triadic' because it posits three main components in sign constitution: the actual physical sign, the thing to which it refers, and the interpretation that it elicits in real-world situations. Peirce called the form a *representamen* ('something that does the representing') and the concept that it encodes the *object* ('something cast outside for observation'). He termed the meaning that we get from it the *interpretant*. This constitutes a 'derived' sign itself, because it entails the further production of meanings arising from the context in which a sign is used. In our culture, a cat is considered to be a domestic companion, among other things; in others it is viewed primarily as a sacred animal (akin to a sacred cow in some societies); and in others still it is considered to be a source of food (cat meat). Thus, while the sign refers to virtually the same mammal in different cultures (not matter what name is used), its interpretant varies considerably, constituting a source of supplementary (and obviously crucial) semiosis.

Peirce also developed a comprehensive typology of signs – a typology that has yet to be eclipsed. He identified sixty-six types in total. Newcomers to semiotics often react with perplexity to his typology, which consists of seemingly obscure and unfathomable notions such as *qualisigns*, *sinsigns*, and *legisigns*. But it is actually quite straightforward. For instance, as its name implies, a *qualisign* is a sign that draws attention to some *quality* of its referent (the object it represents). In language, an adjective is a qualisign since it draws attention to the qualities (colour, shape, size, etc.) of things. In other sign systems, qualisigns include colours (painting), harmonies and tones (music), and so forth. A *sinsign* is a sign that *singles* out a particular object – a pointing finger and the words *here* and *there* are examples of sinsigns. A *legisign* is a sign that designates something by convention (literally 'by law'). Legisigns include various kinds of symbols and emblems such as those used on flags and logos.

Unlike Saussure and much like Plato (§1.2), Peirce viewed semiosis as originating in the perception of some property in an object. For this reason, he called the act of sign creation or sign interpretation a 'firstness' event. Firstness is, more technically, a tendency to forge or interpret signs as simulations of the world. As we shall see in the next chapter, he called this process *iconicity*. Since 'iconic signs' are fashioned in culture-specific contexts, their manifestations across cultures are not exactly alike, even though they spring from the same human perceptual apparatus. Peirce used the term *hypoicon* to acknowledge this culture-constrained dimension of firstness. Nevertheless, because it is a firstness (sensory-based) sign, its referent can be figured out even by those who are not a part of the culture, if they are told how it simulates, resembles, or substitutes it. A 'secondness' tendency in sign creation or sign interpretation consists in relating objects in some way. He called this tendency *indexicality*. The pointing finger is a basic example of a secondness sign, known as an *index*. When we point to something, we are in fact relating it to our location as pointers. If it is close by we refer to it as *near* or *here*. If not, we refer to it as *far* or *there*. Finally, Pierce posited that there exists a 'thirdness' tendency in sign creation or interpretation, which consists in learning and using signs in conventional ways. He called signs that result from this tendency *symbols*. The cross figure used to stand for Christianity is a perfect example of a symbol. Although it represents the figure of the cross on which Christ was crucified, it is interpreted historically and conventionally as a sign standing for the religion that was founded after Christ's death.

Despite the obvious richness and breadth of Peircean sign theory, the Saussurean model continues to have wide usage among semioticians because it is a much more expedient one to apply, especially in the initial phases of analysis. Signifiers can easily be separated from contexts of occurrence and studied abstractly in relation to signifieds, albeit somewhat artificially. Peirce's model, however, has proven to be a more insightful and all-encompassing one in the development of a comprehensive theory of meaning.

1.5 The Current Practice of Semiotics

It is accurate to say that semioticians today use a blend of Saussurean and Peircean concepts and techniques at various stages of analysis and for diverse purposes. They also often use ideas and findings from related or cognate disciplines, especially linguistics, philosophy, psychology, and anthropology. Note, however, that this 'interdisciplinary' mode of inquiry is a two-way street, in that many ideas developed within semiotics proper are now found scattered throughout cognate fields. It was actually Saussure who originated the interdisciplinary orientation of contemporary semiotics by arguing that semiology should be considered a part of psychology and linguistics a part of semiology. His suggestion merits some consideration here, since current semiotic theory and practice is highly interactive with theories and practices in both psychology and linguistics.

Since ancient times, philosophers have wondered what the mind is. Plato and Aristotle believed that it was separate from the body. During the Renaissance, Descartes further entrenched this view – adding, however, that the two strongly influenced each other. He even suggested that the interaction between body and mind takes place in the pineal gland, a tiny organ in the brain.

Psychology was forged as a science independent of philosophy in 1875, the year the American philosopher William James (1842–1910) founded the world's first psychology 'laboratory' to study the mind in a 'scientific,' rather than a speculative (philosophical) manner. A similar laboratory was established in Leipzig by Wilhelm Wundt (1832–1920) in 1879. Wundt, also a philosopher, published the first journal of experimental psychology. James and Wundt both defined psychology as the study of mind through experimentation with human subjects. By the late 1960s, however, a new cadre of psychologists were beginning to question the experimental orientation of their discipline, and seeking to gain insights into the mind by examining parallels between the functions of the human brain and those of computer systems. Computer terms such as 'storage,' 'retrieval,' and 'processing' became part of the emerging new lexicon in psychology, and remain basic ones to this day. This movement led in the 1980s and 1990s to the view that human intelligence itself may be a product of 'computational laws' built into the human brain by evolutionary forces. Some radical evolutionary psychologists, as they are now called, even argue that human consciousness is no more than the outcome of the complex operations of such laws (or principles) developed through evolutionary processes. Contemporary semiotics sees evolutionary processes as interactive with historical ones in generating consciousness. Moreover, it assigns much weight to human inventiveness and creativity as factors shaping human evolution. Semiotics is thus a safeguard against determinism in any of its modern forms.

Modern linguistics is the twin sister of semiotics, since it also traces its parentage to Saussure's *Cours de linguistique générale* (§1.2). Since its birth, linguistics has always aimed to study *langue*, as Saussure called it – namely, the forms and functions of the sounds, words, and grammatical categories of specific languages, as well as the formal relationships that exist among different languages. Early on, though, many linguists also saw the usefulness of studying the everyday use of *langue* (called *parole* by Saussure) in specific social situations. Among the first to do so profitably were Franz Boas (1858–1942) and his student Edward Sapir (1884–1939). Boas and Sapir devised practical field methods for gathering information on unwritten languages – methods that were systematized by the American linguist Leonard Bloomfield (§1.3) in 1933. Their ultimate goal was to understand the links among language (*langue*), discourse (*parole*), and culture. In the 1950s two main branches of linguistics were established to deal directly with *parole*: *sociolinguistics* and *psycholinguistics*. The former aims to describe the kinds of behaviours that correlate with the use of language in different social contexts; the latter is concerned with such issues as language acquisition in childhood, the nature of speech perception, the localization of language in the brain, and the relationship between language and thought. Of special relevance to semiotics is the hypothesis, put forward in the mid-1930s by Edward Sapir's student Benjamin Lee Whorf (1897–1941), that language conditions the specific ways in which people think and act. The question of whether the 'Whorfian Hypothesis' is tenable continues to be debated. If the signs of a particular language system constitute a set of strategies for classifying, abstracting, and storing information in culture-specific ways, do these predispose its users to attend only to certain specific perceptual events and ignore others? If so, do speakers of different languages perceive the world in different ways? These are the kinds of intriguing questions that the Whorfian Hypothesis invites. Much of the contemporary semiotic inquiry into language is, in fact, guided by such questions.

Like psychology and linguistics, semiotics can be characterized as a science. True, meaning cannot be studied with the same objectivity as, say, physical matter is by chemists. Even so, semiotics constitutes a science in the traditional sense of the word for five fundamental reasons, as Umberto Eco has cogently suggested:[9]

1. It is an autonomous discipline.
2. It has a set of standardized methodological tools that allow semioticians to seek answers to specific kinds of questions (What does something mean? How does it mean what it means? Why does it mean what it means?).
3. It has the capacity to generate hypotheses about semiosis, by analysing the products of semiosis.
4. It affords the possibility of making predictions, such as how societies and cultures will evolve through semiosis.
5. Its findings can lead to a modification of the actual state of the objective world.

Needless to say, claims to 'objectivity' need to be tempered with caution. This is not unique to semiotics, however. It has, in fact, become characteristic of all the sciences in the twentieth century ever since Werner Heisenberg (1901–76), the German physicist and Nobel laureate, put forward his now famous *indeterminacy principle* during the first part of the century. This principle debunks the notion that an objective reality exists independent of culture and of the scientist's personal participation in it.

To Eco's list of reasons, I would add a sixth: semiotic inquiry, like inquiry in any other scientific enterprise, is guided by a set of specific axioms. As far as I can surmise, at least seven axioms have guided the semiotician's exploration of meaning over the past century. These can be formulated as follows:

1. Sign systems the world over are constructed with the same innate semiosic tendencies, as Pierce emphasized (simulation, relation, etc.).
2. This implies that there are universal structures of semiosis in the human species that are constrained only by force of history and tradition.
3. Particular sign systems are specific instantiations of these structures.
4. Differences in sign systems result from differences in such instantiations, as caused by human variability and fluctuating contextual-historical factors.
5. Sign systems thus entail culture-specific classifications of the world.
6. These classifications influence the way people think, behave, and act.
7. Perceptions of 'naturalness' are thus tied to sign systems.

In the end, semiotic inquiry aims to understand the quest for meaning to life – a quest so deeply rooted in human beings that it subtly mediates how they experience the world. This quest gains material expression in the signs and sign systems found throughout human societies. Paradoxically, these are highly restrictive and creative at the same time. Signs learned in social contexts are highly selective of what is to be known and memorized from the infinite variety of things that are in the world. By and large, we let our culture (which is a network of signs) 'do the thinking' for us when we use signs unreflectively. But there is a paradox here – a paradox that lies in the fact that we can constantly change, expand, elaborate, or even discard the habits of thought imprinted in sign systems. We do this by creating new signs (words, symbols, etc.) to encode new knowledge and modify previous knowledge. The human species is, above all else, a highly creative and imaginative one.

1.6 Further Reading and Online Resources

Further Reading

Barthes, Roland. *Elements of Semiology*. London: Cape, 1968.

Clarke, D.S. *Principles of Semiotic*. London: Routledge and Kegan Paul, 1987.

Deely, John. *Basics of Semiotics*. Bloomington: Indiana University Press, 1990.

– *Four Ages of Understanding: The First Postmodern Survey of Philosophy from Ancient Times to the Turn of the Twentieth Century*. Toronto: University of Toronto Press, 2001.

Eco, Umberto. *Semiotics and the Philosophy of Language*. Bloomington: Indiana University Press, 1984.

– *A Theory of Semiotics*. Bloomington: Indiana University Press, 1976.

merrell, floyd. *Peirce, Signs, and Meaning*. Toronto: University of Toronto Press, 1997.

– *Signs Grow: Semiosis and Life Processes*. Toronto: University of Toronto Press, 1996.

Morris, Charles W. *Foundations of the Theory of Signs*. Chicago: University of Chicago Press, 1938.

– *Writings on the General Theory of Signs*. The Hague: Mouton, 1946.

Nöth, Winfried. *Handbook of Semiotics*. Bloomington: Indiana University Press, 1990.

Ogden, C.K., and I.A. Richards. *The Meaning of Meaning*. London: Routledge and Kegan Paul, 1923.

Posner, Roland, K. Robering, and Thomas A. Sebeok, eds. *Semiotik/Semiotics. Ein Handbuch zu den zeichentheoretischen Grundlagen von Natur und Kultur / A Handbook on the Sign-Theoretic Foundations of Nature and Culture*. 4 vols. Berlin and New York: Mouton de Gruyter, 1997–2004.

de Saussure, Ferdinand. *Cours de linguistique générale*, ed. C. Bally and A. Sechehaye. Paris: Payot, 1916; trans. W. Baskin, *Course in General Linguistics*. New York: McGraw-Hill, 1958.

Sebeok, Thomas A. *Contributions to the Doctrine of Signs*. Lanham, MD: University Press of America, 1976.

– *I Think I Am a Verb: More Contributions to the Doctrine of Signs*. New York: Plenum, 1986.

– *The Play of Musement*. Bloomington: Indiana University Press, 1981.

– *The Sign and Its Masters*. Austin: University of Texas Press, 1979.

– ed. *Encyclopedic Dictionary of Semiotics*. 3 vols. Berlin, New York, and Amsterdam: Mouton de Gruyter, 1986.

The main journal for research in semiotic theory and practice is *Semiotica*, founded by the International Association of Semiotic Studies in 1969 under the editorship of Thomas A. Sebeok, who remained its editor until his death in 2001. At the time of writing, the author of this book is the current editor. Other major journals that publish ongoing research in semiotic theory are *Sign System Studies, Versus, American Journal of Semiotics, European Journal of Semiotics,* and *Zeitschrift für Semiotik*.

Online Resources

The popular and useful website maintained by Daniel Chandler, *Semiotics for Beginners* (http://www.aber.ac.uk/media/Documents/S4B/sem02.html), is very well written for a general audience. Martin Ryder's website, http://carbon.cudenver.edu/~mryder/martin.html, is a storehouse of information and links related to a vast array of topics in semiotics. An excellent survey of semiotic theory in the medieval period is the one by Stephan Meier-Oeser: http://plato.stanford.edu/entries/semiotics-medieval/.

There is an excellent online journal, *Applied Semiotics* (http://www.chass.utoronto.ca/french/as-sa/index.html), edited by Peter G. Marteinson and Pascal G. Michelucci, which covers a broad range of topics in the theory and practice of semiotics.

2 Signs

Everything ideological possesses meaning: it represents, depicts, or stands for something lying outside itself. In other words, it is a sign. Without signs there is no ideology.

V.N. Volosinov (1905–60)

2.1 Introduction

When we gesture, talk, write, read, watch a TV program, listen to music, look at a painting, we are engaged in primarily unconscious sign-based behaviours of various kinds. As Peirce aptly remarked, human life is characterized above all else by a 'perfusion of signs.' Without them we would have to resort to a purely instinctual form of existence. Perhaps the most important function of signs is that they make knowledge practicable by giving it a physical and thus retrievable and usable form. Although we process information about the world through our sensory apparatus, the cognitive uses of such information would quickly vanish without signs to encode and preserve it in some reusable way. Knowledge is 'signed information.' Modern humans are more a product of semiosis than they are of evolutionary instinctual processes. However, there is a price to pay for all this – the sign systems we acquire in cultural contexts constitute powerful mental and emotional filters for interpreting the world, guiding us constantly in our attempts to grasp the meaning of that very world. That there are dynamic interactions among signs, knowledge, and meaning is a basic axiom of semiotic theory (see §1.5).

Before any attempt at a systematic description or explanation of the nature of this interaction, it is essential, clearly, for us to have at our disposal a consistent and coherent terminology for differentiating among the various types of signs created and used by humans in their different spheres of existence. Imagine chemistry (or any science, for that matter) without an appropriate terminology. The study of physical matter would end up being a highly subjective and anecdotal one indeed, making it a practically useless intellectual endeavour. Similarly, without a basic terminology, studying the role of signs in human life would be solipsistic at best, and utterly pointless at worst. The first task of semiotic science, then, is to identify, name, and classify signs and their functions. Although there are as many as sixty-six distinct types of sign, as Peirce showed (§1.4), these can be grouped into six broad categories – symptoms, signals, icons, indices, symbols, and names – as the late Thomas Sebeok argued.[1] This chapter describes these categories.

2.2 Defining the Sign

The term *sign* has different senses in English. It is used, for example, to designate a traffic signal (as in 'stop sign') or a business premise (as in 'shop sign'). Stop signs and shop signs are not trivial matters to a semiotician. They are 'signs' in the semiotic sense, since people perceive them not as physical objects in themselves, but as standing for something other than themselves. Similarly, the V-sign (§1.1) does not constitute a mere shape made by two fingers; rather, it represents certain social concepts (victory, peace, greeting, femininity, etc.). As these examples suggest, a sign can be defined simply as 'something that stands for something else in some way.'

In order for somebody to recognize 'something' as a sign, however, that 'something' must have *structure* – that is, some distinctive, recognizable, and recurring physical form. As we saw in the previous chapter (§1.4), Saussure referred to this component of sign structure as the signifier. The other component – the 'something else' for which a physical structure stands – is the signified. The connection between the two, once established, is bidirectional or binary – that is, one implies the other. For example, the word *tree* is a word sign in English because it has a recognizable phonetic structure that generates a mental concept (an arboreal plant):

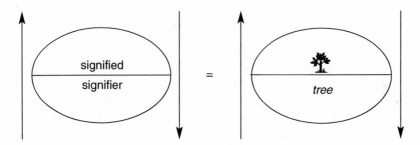

When we utter the word *tree*, the image of an arboreal plant inevitably comes to mind, and in fact, such an image cannot be blocked; vice versa, when we see an arboreal plant, the word *tree* seems to come also automatically to mind. In effect, both components exist in tandem, not separately. This model of the sign traces its origin back to the Scholastics (§1.2), who also viewed the sign (*signum* in Latin) as an identifiable form composed of two parts: a *signans* ('that which does the signifying') and a *signatum* ('that which is signified'). Although the psychological relation that inheres between signs and the concepts they evoke has come under several terminological rubrics, the term *semiosis* is the preferred one today (§1.2).

Saussure argued further that the binary connection established between the physical structure of a sign (the signifier) and its meaning (the signified) is an arbitrary one, developed over time for some specific social purpose. There was no evident reason for using, say, *tree* or *arbre* (French) to designate 'an arboreal plant,' other than to name it as such. Indeed, any well-formed signifier could have been used in either language – *tree* is a well-formed signifier in English; *tbee* is not (for obvious phonetic reasons). Saussure did admit, however, that some signs were fashioned in imitation of some sensory or perceivable property detectable in their referents. Onomatopoeic words (*drip, plop, whack*, etc.), he granted, were indeed put together to simulate real physical sounds. But he maintained that the coinage of such words was the exception, not the rule. Moreover, the highly variable nature of onomatopoeia across languages proved that it was itself a largely arbitrary sign-making process. For instance, the expression used to refer to the sounds made by a rooster is *cock-a-doodle-do* in English, but *chicchirichì* (pronounced 'keekkeereekee') in Italian; and the expression employed to refer to the barking of a dog is *bow-wow* in English, but *ouaoua* (pronounced 'wawa') in French. Obviously, representing what a rooster or a dog sounds like when it crows or barks is largely an arbitrary process, one that depends on culture.

Yet the fact remains that such words are highly suggestive of actual crowing and barking, no matter how different they may seem phonetically. Moreover, Saussure's claim that onomatopoeia is a sporadic and random phenomenon in word-formation does not stand up to closer scrutiny. Many words possess a latent sound-imitative quality built right into their structure. Consider the word *duck*. The combination of sounds used in its make-up is, to be sure, one of an infinite number of permissible phonetic assemblages that can be envisioned in English, as Saussure would have it. But the final /k/ of that word hints at the kind of sound the animal in question is perceived to make. Its use constitutes a case of 'sound modelling.' Such modelling is well known in both linguistics and semiotics, coming under the name of *sound symbolism*. Saussure was obviously unaware of the pervasiveness of sound symbolism in the formation of the basic vocabularies of languages, nor could he have been, since its discovery as a primary force in language origins was made several decades after his death.[2] Here are a few examples of English words whose final consonants model sonorous properties in referents:

Consonants	Words	Sonorous Properties Modelled
/p/	*dip, rip, sip* ...	a quick abbreviated sound
/k/	*crack, click, creak* ...	a sharp truncated or snapping sound
/b/	*rub, jab, blob* ...	an abrupt resonant sound
/l/	*rustle, bustle, trickle* ...	a soft fluttering or crackling sound
/z/	*ooze, wheeze, squeeze* ...	a hissing sound
/f/	*puff, huff, cough* ...	a short, forced sound

In line with sound symbolism theory, it is plausible to infer that the word *duck* was constructed with /k/, rather than some other final consonant, in order to call attention to the actual sounds that a duck is perceived to emit – a feature captured more explicitly by the word *quack*. Although we probably do not experience the word *duck* consciously as a sign 'motivated' in its formation by a sound-modelling process, we certainly seem to feel intuitively that it is better suited to represent the animal in question than alternative word candidates do. (As the old saying goes, 'If it quacks like a duck, it's a duck.') Motivated structures, such as the words created through sound symbolism, have always been of general interest to semioticians because of the insights they provide into the nature of semiosis.

In contrast to Saussure, Peirce saw motivated structure as the 'default' type of structure. As we saw in the previous chapter (§1.4), Peirce called the sign a *representamen* in order to bring out the fact that a sign is something that 'represents' something else in order to suggest it (i.e., 're-present' it) in some way. He defined the representamen as follows:[3] 'A sign, or representamen, is something which stands to somebody for something in some respect or capacity. It addresses somebody, that is, creates in the mind of that person an equivalent sign. That sign which it creates I call the interpretant of the first sign. The sign stands for something, its object not in all respects, but in reference to a sort of idea.'

A key notion in this definition is that a sign invariably generates another sign, or interpretant, which in turn becomes itself a source of additional semiosis. This process does not continue indefinitely, however. Eventually it must resolve itself into a set of forms that allow us to classify and understand the world in a relatively stable fashion. This set, Peirce claimed, generates a system of beliefs that guides our actions and shapes our behaviours unconsciously. Doubt arises when our current beliefs are not accounted for through the set – that is, when the character of signs in the set does not fit our understanding of the experience. To remove doubt, we resort to inference, and this leads, in turn, to new sign creations. Thus, according to Peirce, it is doubt that drives the making of knowledge.

2.3 Symptoms and Signals

As we saw in the previous chapter, since antiquity a basic distinction has always been made between natural and conventional signs. For most of the early and middle part of the twentieth century, the study of natural signs held a minor place in semiotics proper. However, due mainly to the efforts of Thomas A. Sebeok and other members of the biosemiotic movement (§1.5), the study of such signs became an intrinsic part of semiotic theory and practice towards the latter part of the century. This continues to be so.

What is a natural sign? Simply put, it is a sign produced by Nature. Consider *symptoms*. These are natural signs produced by the body to alert an organism to the presence of some altered physical state within it. Symptoms range from painful sensations (such as headaches or backaches), to visible marks (such as swellings or rashes) and changes in body temperature. The bodies of all animals produce characteristic symptoms as warning signs. A cluster of symptoms that collectively exemplify a disease or disorder is called a *syndrome*. A syndrome is, essentially, a composite sign with a fixed meaning. As von Uexküll (§1.3) demonstrated, symptoms and syndromes vary according to species and thus can be used to define a species biologically. The bodies of animals with similar physiological and anatomical structure will produce similar types of symptoms; those with widely divergent anatomical structures will manifest virtually no symptoms in common.

As mentioned, before the biosemiotic movement semioticians tended to exclude symptoms from their purview, viewing them as products of natural processes and thus as bearing little relevance to the study of signs as socially meaningful structures. Barthes, for instance, dismissed symptoms as 'pure signifiers' with no meanings other than physiological ones. Symptoms, he argued, become true signs – signifiers tied to signifieds – only in the context of clinical discourse, when the interpreter of a symptomatic form is a physician or, by extension, a veterinarian. But in actual fact, the interpreter need be none of these. It could, for example, be a speechless creature, since human symptoms are commonly perceived and acted upon by such domesticated animals as dogs and horses, in a variety of situations in which human discourse plays no mediating role.

A type of natural sign studied much more extensively than symptoms by semioticians today is the *signal*. The bodies of all animals produce signals automatically for conveying specific physical needs or simply as reactants to specific stimuli. Birds, for instance, are born prepared to produce a particular type of coo, and no amount of exposure to the songs of other species, or the absence of their own, has any modifying effect on their cooing signals. A bird reared in isolation, in fact, will sing a very simple outline of the sort of song that would develop spontaneously in that bird born in its natural habitat. This does not mean, however, that animal signalling is not subject to environmental conditioning and experience. Many bird species have, in fact, developed location-based cooing 'dialects,' apparently by imitating one another. Similarly, vervet monkeys are born with the ability to use a specific set of signals to express their particular types of needs, but they also have developed a set of situation-based predator calls –

one alerting the group to eagles, one to four-legged predators such as leopards, another to snakes, and one to other primates. These calls are not innate; they are learned through the observation of older monkeys and by trial and error. An infant vervet may at first deliver an aerial alarm to signal a vulture, a stork, or even a falling leaf, but eventually comes to ignore everything airborne except the eagle.

Because animal signals are truly remarkable in themselves, it is little wonder that people are often tricked into reading much more into them in human terms than is actually there. A well-known example of how easily people are duped by animal signalling behaviour is the case of Clever Hans. In 1904, Clever Hans was heralded the world over as a German 'talking horse' because he appeared to understand human language, devising answers to the questions of its trainer by tapping numbers or the alphabet with his front hoof – one tap for the number one or for the letter A, two taps for the number two or the letter B, and so on. A panel of scientists ruled out deception by the horse's trainer. The horse, it was claimed, could talk! Clever Hans was awarded honours and proclaimed an important scientific discovery. Eventually, however, an astute member of the scientific committee that had examined the horse, the Dutch psychologist Oskar Pfungst, started suspecting that Clever Hans would probably not tap his hoof without observing his questioner, since the horse had probably figured out – as most horses can – what the signals that his owner was unwittingly transmitting meant. The horse, Pfungst asserted, tapped his hoof only in response to inadvertent cues from his human handler, who would visibly relax when the horse had tapped his hoof the proper number of times. To show this, Pfungst simply blindfolded Clever Hans, who, as a consequence, ceased to be so clever. The 'Clever Hans Effect,' as it has come to be known in the annals of psychology, has been demonstrated over and over with other animals (e.g., a dog will bark in response to unconscious helping cues emitted by its trainer).

A large portion of communication among humans also unfolds in the form of unconscious instinctive signals. It has been shown, for example, that men are sexually attracted to women with large pupils, because they are felt to convey a strong sexually-tinged interest, besides making females look younger.[4] This fact was obviously known, or at least intuited, by the manufacturer of a popular eye-drop cosmetic used in central Europe during the 1920s and 1930s, which was made with a crystalline alkaloid liquid appropriately called belladonna ('beautiful woman' in Italian). The cosmetic was advertised as enhancing facial appearance and sexual attractiveness by dilating the pupils. But human signalling is not limited to instinctual forms. Humans are capable of deploying signals for social intentions or purposes – for example, nodding, winking, glancing, looking, nudging, kicking, and head tilting are all signals that have conventional sign value in that they encode specific kinds of social meanings. In effect, human semiosis is characterized by a constant interplay among nature, inventiveness, and culture.

The general study of body signals is called *kinesics*. It was first developed by the American anthropologist Ray L. Birdwhistell (1918–94), who used slow-motion films of people interacting during conversations to analyse the body signals that surfaced in them.[5] Birdwhistell borrowed terms and techniques from linguistics to characterize the recurring motions that made up meaningful signalling, in the belief that these motions cohered into a system that was similar to the grammar of language. For this reason, that system came to be called (and continues to be called) 'body language.' Kinesic signals can be innate (unwitting), learned (witting), or a mixture of the two. Blinking, throat clearing, and facial flushing are innate (involuntary) signals, as are facial expressions of happiness, surprise, anger, disgust, and other basic emotions. Laughing, crying, and shrugging the shoulders are examples of mixed signals. They may originate as instinctive actions or behaviours, but cultural rules enter into the picture to shape their structure, timing, and uses. Winking, raising a thumb, and saluting with the hands are all learned signals. Logically, their meanings vary from culture to culture. These signals often accompany vocal speech, imparting a sense to a conversation remembered long after spoken words fade away. Conversely, they can be used to lie or conceal something.

Some kinesic signals have a regulatory function; that is, they are designed to inform people how to behave in certain social situations. Such signals are products of culture and thus largely conventional. Take, for example, the signals used in courtship displays, which range from obsequious laughter to varying forms of kissing and hugging. These may look comical or absurd to outsiders, but to the members of a social group they constitute crucial modes of sexual-romantic communication at key stages in the enactment of courtship. They make sense only if the appropriate social contexts are present during their enactment. So, while courtship displays may be residues of some ancient animal mechanism – as some evolutionary psychologists suggest – the great diversity that is evident in them across cultures indicates that they are not simple biological reflexes, but rather also products of history and tradition. Human signalling systems are the outcome of nature and culture cooperating in a type of partnership that is found nowhere else in the animal realm.

Facial expressions in human beings are other exemplars of this unique partnership. In 1963, psychologist Paul Ekman established the Human Interaction Laboratory in the Department of Psychiatry at the University of California at San Francisco for the purpose of studying facial expressions across the world. He was joined by Wallace V. Friesen in 1965 and Maureen O'Sullivan in 1974. Over the years, work at the laboratory has been crucial in documenting both the universal (biologically based) and cultural forces at work in facial expression.[6] One of the most important findings of the laboratory is that the face is itself a sign – more specifically, a 'sign of Selfhood.' This explains why personality and attractiveness are typically evaluated across cultures on the basis of facial appearance. This is also the most likely reason why humans use facial decorations and make alterations to their faces, especially at crucial stages in their development and maturation. The cosmetics that we use today have, in fact, a long and unbroken connection to ancient courtship practices. From the beginning of time, human beings have made up their faces to convey identity and to make themselves attractive to others.

The eyes have received particular attention from facial researchers because of the central semiotic role they play around the world. Eye contact constitutes a mixed signalling system. Like other species, humans perceive a direct stare as a threat or challenge, and like dogs and primates, they will break eye contact as a signal of surrender. However, many types of eye contact patterns are shaped by culture, not nature. For instance, the length of time involved in eye contact indicates the kind of relationship that exists (or is intended) among people, as does early or late eye contact. This varies, moreover, according to culture. Southern Europeans tend to look more into the other person's eyes during conversation than do North Americans; in some cultures a male does not look into a female's eyes unless he is married to her or is a member of the same family. In many societies, there exists the concept of the 'evil eye,' which is perceived to be a certain kind of stare that is purported to have the power to harm or bewitch someone. No such concept exists in animal species (at least to the best of my knowledge).

Touch patterns are yet another interesting area of kinesic inquiry, falling more specifically under the rubric of *haptics* (from the Greek *haptikos*, 'grasping,' 'touching'). A common social function of touch is greeting. The zoologist Desmond Morris indicates that the Western form of handshaking may have started as a way to show that neither person in the handshake was holding a weapon.[7]

It thus became a 'tie sign' because of the social bonding function it was designed to have. And in fact, handshaking is perceived as a sign of equality among individuals and is often performed to close agreements. Indeed, refusing to shake someone's outstretched hand tends to be interpreted as a 'counter-sign' of aggressiveness or as a challenge. Predictably, haptic greeting behaviours reveal a high degree of cross-cultural variation. Some people squeeze the hand (as Europeans and North Americans do), or shake both hands, or lean forward or stand straight while shaking, and so on. Other haptic forms of communication include patting someone on the arm, shoulder, or back to indicate agreement or praise; linking arms to designate companionship; putting an arm around the shoulder to indicate friendship or intimacy; holding hands to express intimacy; hugging to convey happiness; and so on.

Anthropologists are not sure why haptic forms of communication vary so much across cultures. Perhaps the variation is related to how the body is perceived as a sign of Selfhood. In many parts of the world, people perceive the skin as a surface 'sheath' and the body as a 'container' of the individual's persona. Such people tend to think of themselves as being 'contained' in their bodies and enveloped by their skin.

Others feel instead that the Self is located only within the body shell. Such differences in perception are the sources, arguably, of differential haptic behaviours.[8]

The hands are used not only for haptic or tactile communication but also for gesturing. Although there are cross-cultural similarities in gestures, substantial differences exist regarding both the extent to which gestures are used and the interpretations given to their particular uses. In 1979, Desmond Morris, together with several of his associates at Oxford University, examined twenty gesture signs in forty different areas of Europe.[9] The research team discovered some rather fascinating things. For instance, they found that many of the same gestures had radically different meanings, depending on culture. For example, a tap on the side of the head indicated completely opposite things – 'stupidity' or 'intelligence' – according to culture.

Gestures are not unique to human beings; they are found in primates as well. Chimpanzees raise their arms in the air as a signal that they want to be groomed; they stretch out their arms to beg or invite; and they point to things to indicate their location. Apparently these gestures are purposeful as well as regulatory of the actions of other chimps. But the number of gesture forms of which chimpanzees are capable is limited. Human gesturing, on the other hand, is productive and varied. It is often used to replace vocal speech, as can be seen in its use as a 'sign language' by hearing-impaired people. In American Sign Language (ASL), for instance, the sign for 'catch' is formed with one hand (in the role of agent) moving across the body (an action) to grasp the forefinger of the other hand (the patient). Sign languages are also used for various communicative purposes. One of the best-known examples is the one developed by the Plains people of North America as a means of communication between tribes with different vocal languages. The manual signs represent things in nature, ideas, emotions, and sensations. For example, the sign for a white person is made by drawing two fingers across the forehead, indicating a hat. Special signs exist also for each tribe and for particular rivers, mountains, and other natural features. The sensation of being cold is indicated by a shivering motion of the hands in front of the body; the same sign is used for 'winter' and for 'year,' because the Plains people count years in terms of winters. Slowly turning the hand, relaxed at the wrist, means vacillation, doubt, or possibility; a modification of this sign, with a quicker movement, constitutes a question sign.

Gestures are also used for sacred purposes; this points to the symbolic value of purposeful hand movements. For example, in Christianity the 'sign of the cross' is a gesture intended to represent the central event of Christianity – the Crucifixion. In Buddhism gestures known as *Mudras* are used during ceremonies to represent meditation, reasoning, protection, entreaty, enlightenment, unification of matter, and spirit. The 'devil's hand,' made by raising the index and little fingers, belongs to the domain of superstition, symbolizing, in some cultures, a horned figure intended to ward off the evil eye, in others a sign of 'cuckoldry,' and in still others, 'F--- you.'

Gesture is a more instinctive form of communication than is vocal language. When we do not speak the language of our interlocutor, we instinctively resort to gesture in order to get a message across or to negotiate some meaning. For example, when we want to refer to an automobile, we can use our hands to portray a steering wheel and the back-and-forth motion used to steer a car, accompanying this gesture, perhaps, with an imitative motor sound. This instinctive type of interactive behaviour suggests that gesture is a more basic mode of communication than vocal language. Some truly fascinating research by the American linguist David McNeill has shown, moreover, that gesture is a complement to vocal language.[10] McNeill videotaped a large number of people as they spoke, gathering a substantial amount of data on the gesture signs that accompany speech, which he termed *gesticulants*. His findings suggest that these are used in tandem with words because they exhibit images that cannot be communicated overtly in speech. In psychological terms, they are traces to what the speaker is thinking about. Speech and gesticulation, it would seem, constitute a single integrated communication system in which both cooperate to express the person's meanings.

McNeill identified five main types of gesticulants. First, there are iconic gesticulants, which (as their name suggests) bear a close resemblance to the referents of words and sentences. For example, when describing a scene from a story in which a character bent a tree back to the ground, one speaker that McNeill observed performed a 'gripping' gesture as if grasping something and pulling it back and down. The speaker's gesticulant was, in effect, a simulation of the action he was describing vocally, revealing both his mental image of the action and his point of view (he could have taken the part of the tree instead). Second, McNeill identified metaphoric gesticulants, which are also pictorial but much more abstract in form than their iconic counterparts. For example, McNeill recorded a male speaker recounting his recollection of a certain cartoon, raising up his hands as he did so, as if offering his listeners a kind of object. The speaker was clearly not referring to the cartoon itself, but rather to the genre, as if it were an object that he intended to offer as a gift to his listeners. This type of gesticulant typically accompanies utterances that contain expressions such as 'presenting an idea,' 'putting forth an idea,' 'offering advice,' and so on. Third, McNeill observed speakers using hand movements that resembled the beating of musical tempo. He called these, logically, beat gesticulants, since they accompany the rhythmic pulsation of speech, usually in the form of a simple flick of the hand or of fingers moving up and down or back and forth. Beat gesticulants mark the introduction of new ideas or characters in a story; that, or they accompany summaries or rundowns. Fourth, McNeill recorded hand movements designed to show how the separate parts of an utterance are supposed to hold together. He named these cohesive gesticulants. They are performed typically through a repetition of the same hand action. It is the repetition itself that is meant to convey cohesiveness. Fifth, McNeill noted that speakers often used pointing movements, which he called deictic. Such gesticulants are aimed not at an existing physical place, but rather at an abstract concept that was introduced earlier in the conversation.

McNeill's gesticulant categories are actually subtypes of the more generic category of gestures known as *illustrators*. Four other categories have been identified by gesture researchers. They are as follows:

Emblems. These are gestures used to translate words or phrases. Examples: the *okay* sign, the *come here* sign, the hitchhiking sign, waving, and obscene gestures.

Affect displays. These communicate emotional meaning. Examples: the hand actions and movements that accompany expressions of happiness, surprise, fear, anger, sadness, contempt, or disgust.

Regulators. These are designed to regulate or control the speech of
someone else. Examples: the hand movements for *keep going, slow
down,* and *What else happened?*

Adaptors. These indicate some need or state of mind. Examples:
scratching the head when puzzled, rubbing the forehead when
worried.

2.4 Icons

Conventional signs are those made by human beings for their particular intellectual, cognitive, emotional, aesthetic, and social needs. How
are they made? Are there any general patterns noticeable in the construction process? It was Peirce who answered these questions in an
insightful way, pointing out that humans create signs in accordance
with three general psychological tendencies: resemblance, relation,
and convention. He called signs resulting from resemblance *icons,*
those from relation *indexes,* and those from convention *symbols.*

Icons can be defined simply as signs that have been constructed to
resemble their referents in some way. Photographs, portraits, and
Roman numerals such as I, II, and III are visual icons because they
resemble their referents in a visual way. Onomatopoeic words such as
drip, plop, bang, and *screech* are vocal icons created to simulate the
sounds that certain things, actions, or movements are perceived to
make. Perfumes are olfactory icons manufactured to imitate natural
scents. Chemical food additives are gustatory icons simulating the taste
of natural foods. A block with a letter of the alphabet carved into it is a
tactile icon allowing the user to figure out the letter through the
medium of touch. Peirce called the actual referent that is modelled in a
direct way the 'immediate' object; the infinite number of referents that
can be modelled in similar ways he termed the 'dynamical' objects.

It is relevant to note that before Peirce began using the term in semiotics, *icon* was employed to refer to a religious painting, sculpture, or
token. It is still used with this meaning today. In some religions the
religious icon is thought to be sacred and thus to aid believers in con-
tacting the represented figure. Beginning in the eighth century, *icono-
clasm,* a movement that condemned the worship of icons as idolatrous,
contributed to the destruction of much religious iconic art throughout
the Byzantine Christian world. Not until the following century was the
making of icons restored to its former position of honour in many
kinds of religious observances.

Iconicity (or the making of iconic signs) is simulative semiosis. It is
evidence that human understanding is guided initially by sensory per-

ception and is thus sensitive to recurrent patterns of colour, shape, dimension, movement, sound, taste, and so on. Put simply, humans tend to model the world as they see, hear, smell, taste, and touch it. The prehistoric inscriptions, cave drawings, and pictographic signs of humanity indicate that iconicity played an important role in early sign systems and cultures. The earliest of these go back more than thirty thousand years. They took two main forms: the vivid paintings of animals that today still cover the roofs and walls of caves, such as Lascaux in France and Altamira in Spain; and the small sculptures and relief carvings of animals and female figures found in caves throughout Europe. The anthropologist Denise Schmandt-Besserat has shown that the earliest precursors of modern writing systems were such carvings and figures. A number have been discovered as well in western Asia dating back to the Neolithic era.[11]

Iconicity also marks early learning behaviours. Children invariably pass through an initial stage of imitative gesticulation and imitative vocalism before they develop full verbal language. It is relevant to note that although the latter eventually becomes the dominant form of communication in humans, the gestural and vocalic modalities do not vanish completely. Throughout life, they remain functional subsystems of human communication that can always be utilized as more generic forms when linguistic interaction is impossible or limited. Iconicity also shows up in the instinctive desire of children to make scribbles and elemental drawings at about the same time they utter their first true words. If given drawing materials around the age of one or two, children impulsively start scribbling on any available surface. As time passes, their scribbles become more and more controlled; geometrical shapes such as crude circles, crosses, and rectangles, at first accidentally produced, are repeated and gradually perfected. Although children, with adult prompting, may learn to label circles as 'suns' or 'faces,' they do not seem inclined at first to name them in any way. The act of making shapes appears to be pleasurable and satisfying in itself. Of course, shapes eventually suggest 'things' to the child as his or her ability to use language for naming purposes develops; but in the beginning, the child seems to engage in drawing solely for the pleasure of it, without attaching explicit associations of meaning to it. It is truly an example of 'art for art's sake.'

In the adult world, iconicity serves a vast range of social functions. Pictures on washroom doors representing males and females, for example, are independent of language and thus much more universally understood. And vocalism is an inbuilt feature of language whether we realize it or not. Vocalism can be defined, simply, as the use of sounds to model something through imitation or resemblance, or to emphasize or call attention to something. Vocalism manifests itself in such common linguistic phenomena as these:

- Alliteration, or the repetition of initial sounds, for various imitative effects. Examples: *ding-dong, no-no*.
- Sound lengthening and intonation to simulate emotions. Examples: *Yesssss! Noooooo!*
- Sound symbolism (§2.2), which can be seen, for example, in the sound-modelling language of comic books: *Zap! Boom! Pow!*
- Onomatopoeia. For example, describing a snake as *slithery* or *slippery*, in imitation of the sounds that snakes are perceived to make.
- Increasing or decreasing loudness levels during vocal delivery in order to convey, for example, anger or excitement or their opposites (calmness, composure).
- Increasing the rate of speech to simulate (for example) urgency or agitation, and decreasing it to convey the opposite states (placidness or indolence).

Iconicity is also a factor in the construction of diagrams in mathematics and science. In mathematics, for instance, diagrams modelling the given conditions (called *heuristic devices)* are often used to make problems more understandable. If a problem says that A is taller than B and that C is taller than A and then asks us to identify who the tallest is, the following diagram, which constitutes a picture of the given information in outline form, can help make the problem more understandable:

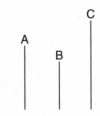

The diagram reveals to the eye that C is the tallest. Many diagrams used in science to model physical phenomena – such as the model of the atom as a miniature cosmos – are iconic in nature.

Today the term *icon* is often used to designate a tiny picture on a computer screen representing a command. The icons, cursor, and mouse together constitute what is called a *graphical user interface* (GUI), a system that provides a user-friendly way of interacting with a computer. People can usually tell from icons how to get the computer to do what they want. Without a GUI, the computer screen would be black, and the only way to tell the computer what to do would be to type in commands. There is little doubt that GUIs contributed to the rise in use of personal computers, starting in 1984, when Apple introduced the Macintosh, the first personal computer to include a GUI. GUIs quickly became standard throughout the computer industry. Today, most users encounter only GUI-based programs and never have to type in commands to control their computers.

As a final word, iconicity is not limited to human semiosis. Indeed, it manifests itself in the cross-species propensity to engage in camouflage, the phenomenon whereby some aspect of a species' physical appearance undergoes changes that make it seem to be part of its surroundings. For instance, the adult females of scale insects (*Icerya purchasi* and *Quadraspidiotus perniciosus*) attach themselves by their mouth parts to plant and tree surfaces, secreting a waxy substance that makes them appear to be part of those surfaces. The common leaf insect (*Phyllidae*) has the capacity to enlarge its legs and abdomen so as to make itself resemble leaves. Similarly, any of several species of long-horned grasshoppers called katydids (*Tettigoniidae*) use their broad wings to blend in with leaves in their environment. Sometimes a creature even has the capacity to fabricate a number of dummy copies of itself so as to misdirect predators away from its body to one of the copies. This capacity is possessed, for instance, by various species of a genus of spiders known as orb-weavers.

2.5 Indexes

An *index* is a sign that involves relation of some kind. Unlike icons, which are constructed to resemble things, indexes are designed to place referents in relation to one another, to sign-users, or to the context or contexts in which they occur. A perfect example of an indexical sign is the pointing index finger, which we use instinctively from birth to point out and locate things, people, and events. This sign emphasizes, again, the importance of the hands in knowledge making and communication. Many words, too, have an indexical function – for example, *here, there, up,* and *down* allow speakers of English to refer to the relative location of things when speaking about them.

There are four main types of indexes:

1. *Location indexes.* These relate referents to sign users in spatial contexts. Manual signs like the pointing index finger, demonstrative words such as *this* or *that,* adverbs of place like *here* or *there,* figures such as arrows, and maps of all types are common examples of location indexes. Essentially, these allow sign users to indicate their physical location with respect to something (*near, far, here, there,* etc.), or else to indicate the relative location of some referent in spatial terms.

2. *Temporal indexes.* These relate referents to one another in terms of time. Adverbs such as *before, after, now,* and *then,* timeline graphs representing points in time, time units (days, hours, minutes, etc.), and dates on calendars are all examples of temporal indexes.

3. *Identification indexes.* These relate the participants involved in a specific situation or context to one another. Personal pronouns such as *I, you, he, she,* or *they* or indefinite pronouns such as *the one,* or *the other* are examples of identification indexes. So are surnames (which identify individuals in terms of ethnic and familial membership).[12]

4. *Organizational indexes.* These allow us to organize, classify, or categorize things in relation to one another or to other things. The arrangement of books in alphabetical order on library shelves is a perfect example of what organizational indexicality allows us to do. In mathematics, an organizational index – such as a number or symbol written as a subscript or superscript – can indicate an operation to be performed, an ordering relation, or the use of an associated expression.

Indexicality is behind several diagramming techniques. For example, flow chart diagrams and the algorithms employed in mathematics and computer science to indicate the procedures required to perform a task are indexical in nature. So are the time-line diagrams used by scientists to portray temporal relations. DNA profiling diagrams, used in forensic investigations, are also indexical. DNA profiling is a method of identification that compares fragments of deoxyribonucleic acid (DNA), the genetic material found within the cell nuclei of all living things. Except in cases of identical siblings, the complete DNA of each individual is unique. A DNA 'fingerprint' is constructed by first extracting a DNA sample from body tissue or fluid. This is then segmented using enzymes. The segments are marked with probes and exposed on X-ray film, where they form a pattern of black bars. These constitute the fingerprint, which is an identification index. When the fingerprints produced from two different samples match, the samples must have come from the same person.

2.6 Symbols

A *symbol* is a sign that stands for something in a conventional way. For example, the cross figure stands for 'Christianity,' the V-sign for 'peace,' white for 'purity,' and dark for 'impurity.' These symbols have meaning in specific ways. Symbols are the building blocks of social systems. For example, all societies have national symbols. Familiar symbols of the United States include Uncle Sam and the Statue of Liberty. Symbols for other countries include the Maple Leaf for Canada, John Bull for England, and the *fleur-de-lis* for France. Political parties also use symbols for identification purposes. In the United States, a donkey symbolizes the Democratic Party and an elephant the Republican Party. Artefacts such as coats of arms, flags, heraldic emblems, university seals, and the like are symbolic signs of specific kinds. Known more specifically as *emblems,* they indicate membership or ownership. Certain symbols serve as shorthand forms for recording and recalling information. Every branch of science has its own symbols. Thus, in astronomy a set of ancient symbols is used to identify the sun, the moon, the planets, and the stars; in mathematics, Greek letters are used to represent certain constants and variables; and so on.

A perfect illustration of symbolism can be found in the use of colours to refer to various abstract concepts. Take, for example, the symbolic meanings associated with the colours red, blue, and green in English. These are understandable only to those who know English colour terminology and the symbolism it encodes:

red

red carpet treatment ('preferential treatment')
into the red ('in debt')
red herring ('something used to draw attention away from the real
   issue')

red light district ('area of a city with sexual activities and places such as brothels')
red tape ('overly bureaucratic')

blue

the blues ('type of music')
once in a blue moon ('rarely')
true blue ('loyal')
blue funk ('rut')

green

green envy ('great envy')
greenhorn ('inexperienced person')
green thumb ('having the ability to grow things in a garden')

   Interestingly, symbolism is not absent from other species. A rhesus monkey, for instance, shows fear by carrying its tail stiffly out behind. Baboons convey fear by carrying a vertical tail. Such behaviours are clearly symbolic, even though they are different from the type of symbolism that is involved in human behaviours and rituals. The behaviour of the insects of the carnivorous family *Empididae* is similarly symbolic, again in a specific kind of way. In a species of dipterans of this family, the male offers the female an empty balloon prior to copulation. The evolutionary origin of this seemingly bizarre gesture has been unravelled by biologists – it reduces the probability that the male himself will fall prey to his female partner. But the fact remains that the gift of an empty balloon is a symbolic act.

2.7 Names

Names are signs that have both indexical and symbolic value: they are indexical in that they identify a person in some relational way (in relation to a kinship group, to a particular social context, etc.), and they are symbolic in that they are based on specific cultural traditions. The study of *names* falls under a branch of both semiotics and linguistics called *onomastics* (from Greek *onoma*, 'name').
   In Anglo-American culture, given (or first) names can stand for such things as a month or object (*May, June, Ruby, Daisy*), a religious figure

(John, Mary), popular contemporary personalities *(Elvis, Angelina)*, or classical mythic personages *(Diana, Jason)*, among many others. Until the late Middle Ages, one personal name was generally sufficient as an identifier. Duplications, however, began to occur so often that additional differentiations became necessary. Hence, *surnames* were assigned to individuals (literally 'names on top of names'). These were at first either indexical, in that they identified the individual in terms of place of origin or parentage (descendancy), or descriptive, in that they identified the individual in terms of some personal or social feature (e.g., occupation). For example, in England a person living near or at a place where apple trees grew might have been called 'Mary who lives nearby where the apples grow,' hence, *Mary Appleby*. Surnames such as *Woods, Moore, Church*, and *Hill* have been coined in a similar way. Descriptive surnames such as *Black, Short, Long*, and so forth were coined instead to highlight various characteristics of individuals. Descendant surnames were often constructed by prefixation – for example *Mac-*, or *Mc-* in Scottish or Irish names, or *Ap-* in Welsh names – or by suffixation – for example, *-son* in English surnames and *-sen* in Scandinavian surnames *(Johnson* or *Jensen*, 'son of John,' *Maryson*, 'son of Mary,' *Jakobsdottir*, 'daughter of Jacob'). Surnames describing a person's occupation – *Smith, Farmer, Carpenter, Tailor, Weaver*, and so on – also assumed identifier function in the medieval period.

Among the first known people to use more than one name were the ancient Chinese. The Emperor Fuxi is said to have decreed the use of family names about 2852 BCE. The Romans initially used only single names, but later started using three: (1) the *praenomen*, which stood first as the person's given name; (2) the *nomen*, which indicated the *gens*, or clan, to which the person belonged; and (3) the last name, or *cognomen*, which designated the family. A person sometimes added a fourth name, the *agnomen*, to commemorate an illustrious action or remarkable event in his or her life. Family names gained widespread use in northern Italy in the late tenth century. Nobles were the first to adopt them, in order to set themselves apart from common people, and passed them on to their children. A family name thus became the mark of a well-bred person, and so all classes of people aspiring to ascend the social ladder began adopting this practice as well.

In traditional African societies, the circumstances at time of birth (time of day, birth order, and the parents' reaction to the birth) influence the act of name giving. Names such as *Mwanajuma* ('Friday'), *Esi*

('Sunday'), *Khamisi* ('Thursday'), and *Wekesa* ('harvest time') refer to the day or time when the child was born. *Mosi* ('first born'), *Kunto* ('third born'), and *Nsonowa* ('seventh born') are names given to acknowledge the birth order of the newborn. And *Yejide*, ('image of the mother'), *Dada* ('curly hair'), and *Zuberi* ('strong') are names reflecting the parents' reactions to the newborn.

Names are perceived throughout the world to be much more than simple 'identifier signs.' They are laden with all kinds of symbolic meaning. Across cultures, a neonate is not considered a full-fledged member of society until he or she is given a name. The act of naming newborn infants is, in fact, a semiotic rite of admission into society. The ancient Egyptians believed that a name was a living part of an individual, shaping him or her throughout the life cycle and even beyond. They also believed that if an individual's name was forgotten on earth, the deceased would have to undergo a second death. To avoid this danger, names were written multiple times on walls, tombs, and papyri. Political rulers would sometimes erase the names of past monarchs as a means of rewriting history in their favour, since removal of a person's name meant the extinction of the person from memory. In Hebrew culture, the ancient art of *gematria* was based on the belief that the letters of any name could be interpreted as digits and rearranged to form a number containing secret messages encoded in it. The Romans, too, thought that names were prophetic, believing that *nomen est omen* (a 'name is an omen'). Would the Roman view explain names such as Cecil Fielder, who was a fielder in baseball, Rollie Fingers, who was a pitcher, William Wordsworth, who was a poet, Francine Prose, who was a novelist, and Mickey Bass, who was a musician? Perhaps such occurrences simply indicate that some people are inspired subliminally by their names to gravitate towards occupations suggested by them.

Naming trends are remarkably stable in most societies. This is because names link people to culture and tradition. However, in contemporary Western societies, temporary fashion trends often play a role in name giving. This notwithstanding, the trends are never really far-fetched. According to the U.S. Social Security Administration, one-quarter of the top twenty names given in 2004 in America were the same as those given way back in 1880. The top five names for girls and boys in the two eras, according to that governmental agency, are as follows:

Girls
    1880 Mary, Anna, Emma, Elizabeth, Minnie
    2004 Emily, Emma, Madison, Olivia, Hannah
Boys
    1880 John, William, James, Charles, George
    2004 Jacob, Michael, Joshua, Matthew, Ethan

In 1880 the top twenty boys' names were given to more than half of all the boys born; in 2004 they were given to around 20 per cent. The top twenty girls' names were given to around 34 per cent of all girls born in 1880; in 2004 they were given to 14 per cent. Among the ostensible reasons for this differential pattern is that families are smaller today. Nevertheless, the names given today, even in a highly trendy pop culture milieu such as ours, tend in the end to be those that are consistent with tradition.

Interestingly, many animals use signals that have comparable naming functions (at least as we humans interpret them). In birds, for example, it has been found that when partners are absent, the remaining bird will use the sounds normally reserved for the partner, with the result that the partner will return as quickly as possible.[13] Whales emit clicks that seem to have the same purpose of beckoning a partner to come back speedily.

2.8 Further Reading and Online Resources

Further Reading

Barbieri, Marcello, ed. *Introduction to Biosemiotics: The New Biological Synthesis.* Dordrecht: Springer, 2007.

Birdwhistell, Ray L. *Introduction to Kinesics: An Annotation System for Analysis of Body Motion and Gesture.* Louisville: University Press of Kentucky, 1952.

Ekman, Paul. *Emotions Revealed.* New York: Holt, 2003.

– *Telling Lies.* New York: Norton, 1985.

Ekman, Paul, and Wallace Friesen. *Unmasking the Face.* Englewood Cliffs, NJ: Prentice-Hall, 1975.

Morris, Desmond. *The Human Zoo.* London: Cape, 1969.

Morris, Desmond, et al. *Gestures: Their Origins and Distributions.* London: Cape, 1979.

Nuessel, Frank. *The Study of Names: A Guide to the Principles and Topics.* Westport, CT: Greenwood, 1992.

Peirce, Charles S. *Collected Papers of Charles Sanders Peirce*. Ed. C. Hartshorne and P. Weiss. 8 vols. Cambridge, MA: Harvard University Press, 1931–1958.

de Saussure, Ferdinand. *Cours de linguistique générale*. Paris: Payot, 1916.

Schmandt-Besserat, Denise. *Before Writing*. 2 vols. Austin: University of Texas Press, 1992.

– 'The Earliest Precursor of Writing.' *Scientific American* 238 (1978): 50–9.

Sebeok, Thomas A. *Signs: An Introduction to Semiotics*. Toronto: University of Toronto Press, 2001.

Sebeok, Thomas A., and Marcel Danesi. *The Forms of Meaning: Modeling Systems Theory and Semiotics*. Berlin: Mouton de Gruyter, 2000.

Todorov, Tzvetan. *Theories of the Symbol*. Ithaca, NY: Cornell University Press, 1982.

Wheeler, Wendy. *The Whole Creature: Complexity, Biosemiotics, and the Evolution of Culture*. London: Lawrence & Wishart, 2006.

Online Resources

A good website for information on biosemiotics is that of the International Society for Biosemiotic Studies (http://www.biosemiotics.org). For more information on Saussure, the website http://www.revue-texto.net/Saussure/Saussure is recommended; and for Peirce, the Pierce Society site is recommended (http://www.peircesociety.org). The *Sites of Significance for Semiotics* (http://www.chass.utoronto.ca/french/as-sa/EngSem1) is also very useful for its linkages to other websites that deal with sign typologies.

3 Structure

Style and structure are the essence of a book; great ideas are hogwash.
Vladimir Nabokov (1899–1977)

3.1 Introduction

What constitutes a word? Consider the English word *yellow*. We recognize it as a legitimate word because it is composed of sounds (known as *phonemes*) that are connected to each other in a way that is consistent with how English words in general are formed. On the other hand, we would not recognize the form *çeñ* as an acceptable English word, because it contains two phonemes, represented by the alphabet characters *ç* and *ñ*, that do not exist in the set of English phonemes. Nor would we consider *gpeen* to be an authentic word, even though each of its sounds is an authentic English phoneme. The reason in this case is that the sequence *gp* does not occur in English at the beginning of words. In sum, we recognize *yellow* as a 'linguistically correct' word because it possesses English word structure – that is, it is made up of genuine English phonemes that have been linked together in an appropriate sequential fashion. It is an entity whose separate parts form a recognizable structure.

All signs, sign systems, and texts exhibit structure. In music, for example, the arrangement of tones into melodies is felt to be 'musically correct' only if it is consistent with harmonic structure; in clothing fashion, the type and combination of dress items put on the body is felt to be 'sartorially correct' only if it is consistent with the rules of dress that are operative in a certain social situation; and so on. In all these examples, it can be seen that structural appropriateness involves differentiation and combination in tandem. In effect, in order to recognize something as a sign, one must (1) be able to differentiate it from other signs; and (2) know how its component parts fit together. More technically, a sign is a sign if it has both *paradigmatic* (differential) and *syntagmatic* (combinatory) structure.

The notion of structure is so central to semiotic theory and practice that the term *structuralism* is often used as a synonym for the discipline. The same term is used in linguistics and psychology, where it is also a crucial notion. The fact that certain forms, such as words and melodies, bear meaning by virtue of the fact that they have a specific type of structure suggests that they probably mirror internal sensory, emotional, and intellectual structures. To put it another way, humans seem to be programmed to produce and seek structure in the world on the basis of how they themselves are constituted. As the great American writer Henry Miller (1891–1980) aptly put it, the 'world has not to be put in order; the world is order incarnate. It is for us to put ourselves in unison with this order.'[1]

This chapter will look at what the notion of structure entails for semiotic theory and practice generally. At the end, it will also take a brief look at the movement known as *post-structuralism,* which emerged in the middle part of the twentieth century in reaction to the more rigid ideas and practices of structuralist semioticians.

3.2 Paradigmatic and Syntagmatic Structure

What keeps two words, such as *cat* and *rat*, recognizably distinct? It is, in part, the fact that the phonetic difference between initial c (= /k/) and r (= /r/) is perceived as distinctive. This distinctiveness constitutes a *paradigmatic* feature of the two words. Similarly, a major and minor chord of the same key are perceived as distinct on account of a half-tone difference in the middle note of the chord; the left and right shoes of a pair are perceived as distinct because of their different orientations; and so on and so forth.

As such examples bring out, forms are recognizable as meaning-bearing structures in part through a perceivable difference built into some aspect of their physical constitution – a minimal difference in sound, a minimal difference in tone, a minimal difference in orientation, and so on. The psychological importance of this structural feature was noticed first by the psychologists Wilhelm Wundt (1832–1920) and

Edward B. Titchener (1867–1927), who termed it *opposition*. Saussure saw opposition as an intrinsic property of linguistic structure. His insight remains a basic one to this day, guiding a large part of semiotic and linguistic analysis. The linguist determines the meaning and grammatical function of a form such as *cat* by opposing it to another word such as *rat*. This will show, among other things, that the initial consonants /k/ and /r/ are important in English for differentiating the meanings of words. From such oppositions the linguist establishes, one or two features at a time, what makes the word *cat* unique, pinpointing what *cat* means by virtue of how it is different from other words such as *rat, hat,* and so on.

Traditionally, the technique of opposition has been carried out in a *binary* fashion – that is, it has been performed on two forms (e.g., *cat* vs *rat*) at a time. Because binary opposition was used extensively and unreflectively within both semiotics and linguistics in the first part of the twentieth century, to the virtual exclusion of any other kind of analytical technique, it was bound to come under criticism. As we saw in the first chapter (§1.3), by the late 1950s the semantic differential was coming forward to show that oppositions involve gradations or scales. At around the same time, the semiotician Greimas (§1.2) was introducing the concept of the 'semiotic square' which, he contended, was more suitable as a differentiation technique because it involved two sets of oppositions forming a square arrangement. Given a sign s_1 (e.g., *rich*), we determine its overall meaning by opposing it to its contradictory -s_1 (*not rich*), its contrary s_2 (*poor*), and its contradictory -s_2 (*not poor*):

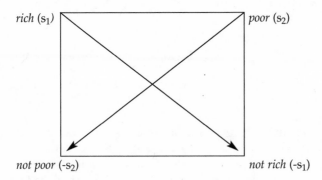

As the semantic differential and semiotic square techniques both suggest, there may be levels and scales of opposition that shape how we recognize signs. According to the anthropologist Claude Lévi-

Strauss, moreover, pairs of oppositions seem to cohere into sets forming recognizable units. In analysing kinship systems, for instance, Lévi-Strauss found that the elementary unit of kinship comprises a set of four oppositions: *brother* vs *sister*, *husband* vs *wife*, *father* vs *son*, and *mother's brother* vs *sister's son*.[2] Lévi-Strauss posited that similar sets underpin units in other cultural systems and, thus, that their study would provide fundamental insights into the overall nature of human social organization.

Generally speaking, the notion of opposition emphasizes the fact that signs have value only in relation to other signs. The relation can be binary, as are phonemic oppositions in language (*cat* vs *rat*); it can be four-part, as are some semantic distinctions (*rich–not rich–poor–not poor*); it can be 'graduated,' as the semantic differential technique has shown with respect to connotative meaning; or it can be cohesive (set based) as anthropologists such as Lévi-Strauss have discovered. These types of opposition are not mutually exclusive, as some have argued in the past. They are, in effect, complementary. It follows that the type of opposition that applies in paradigmatic analysis depends on which system (language, kinship, etc.) or subsystem (phonemic, semantic, etc.) is involved.

Paradigmatic structure, as already noted, tells only part of the semiotic story of how we recognize signs. The other part is syntagmatic structure (§3.1). Take again the words *cat* and *rat* as cases in point. These are legitimate English words, not only because they are recognizable as phonetically distinct through a simple binary opposition of initial phonemes, but also because the combinations of phonemes with which they are constructed are consistent with English syllable structure. On the other hand, *pfat* is not recognizable as a legitimate word in English because it violates an aspect of such structure – English words cannot start with the cluster *pf*. Syllable structure is an example of syntagmatic structure, which characterizes the constitution of signs in all semiotic systems – in music, a melody is recognizable as such only if the notes follow one another in a certain way (e.g., according to the rules of classical harmony); two shoes are considered to form a pair if they are of the same size, style, and colour; and so on.

Differentiation co-occurs with combination. When putting together a simple sentence, for example, we do not choose the words in a random fashion, but rather according to their differential and combinatory properties. The choice of the noun *boy* in the subject slot of a sentence such as *That boy loves pizza* is a paradigmatic one, because other nouns of the same kind – *girl, man, woman,* and so forth – could have been chosen instead and the overall structure of the sentence would have been maintained. This paradigmatic feature of sentence formation can be shown as follows:

	boy		
	girl		
That	man	loves	pizza.
	woman		
	person		
	...		

But the choice of any one of these nouns for that slot constrains the type – *love* vs *drink* – and form – *loves* vs *loving* – of the verb that can be chosen and combined with it. Co-occurrence is a structural feature of all systems. A note chosen to make up a major chord, for instance, must be either the tonic, the median, or the dominant – if it is the tonic, then the other two must be the median and the dominant; if it is the median, then the other two must be the tonic and the dominant; and if it is the dominant, then the other two must be the tonic and the median.

In summary, a sign can be viewed as the result of two intersecting semiotic axes, a vertical one (paradigmatic) and a horizontal one (syntagmatic). Like the coordinates that locate points on the Cartesian plane, they underlie the recognition of a form as a sign. The Cartesian plane is a plane divided into four quadrants by two axes crossing at right angles, the so-called *x*-and *y*-axes. Their point of intersection is known as the origin:

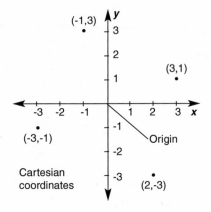

Cartesian coordinates

The point (3, 1), for instance, is defined by its location with respect to these two axes – that is, it is located three equally calibrated units to the right of the y-axis and one unit up from the x-axis; the point (2, -3) is located two units to the right of the y-axis and three units down from the x-axis; the point (-3, -1) is located three units to the left of the y-axis and one unit down from the x-axis; and the point (-1, 3) is located one unit to the left of the y-axis and three units up from the x-axis. In this system, points are defined in relation to one another in terms of such coordinates. Analogously, signs are defined by their paradigmatic and syntagmatic coordinates, so to speak.

3.3 Associative Structure

Consider this sentence: 'The professor is a snake.' What does it mean, really? And how do we get the meaning that we end up extracting from it, since it would seem to make no sense when its words are considered individually? This type of sentence reveals that there is another kind of structure that guides how we link forms together and extract meaning from them. It is called, generally, *associative structure*. Recent work on metaphorical statements such as the one above has revealed that associative structure plays a crucial role in how we derive abstract meanings from sentences and utterances. Associative structure is not equivalent to syntagmatic structure, as some theorists contend. For one thing, it is not constrained structurally, as is, for example, the syntagmatic choice of a verb in a sentence by the co-presence of a specific kind of subject. Rather, it is a type of linkage made by inferring a commonality in meaning among seemingly disparate concepts.

Associative structure occurs in all meaning domains, cutting across sign systems. However, nowhere does it manifest itself as conspicuously as it does in metaphorical language. Consider again: 'The professor is a snake.' In this statement there are two referents: (1) the 'professor' referent, called the *topic* (or *tenor*); and (2) the 'snake' referent, termed the *vehicle*. The linkage of the two creates a type of meaning, called the *ground*, that is much more than the simple sum of the meanings of the two referents. And it is not the denotative meaning of the vehicle that is associated with the topic, but rather its connotative (cultural) meanings as a dangerous reptile. The question now becomes this: Is there any psychological motivation for linking these two referents? The probable reason seems to be an unconscious perception that human personalities and animal behaviours are linked in some way.

In their groundbreaking 1980 book *Metaphors We Live By*, the linguist

George Lakoff and the philosopher Mark Johnson were among the first to argue that associative structure forms the backbone of human understanding.[3] According to traditional accounts of language in philosophy and linguistics, an individual would try out a literal interpretation first when he or she came across a sentence such as 'The professor is a snake,' choosing a metaphorical one only when a literal interpretation was not possible from the context. But as Lakoff and Johnson convincingly demonstrated, this is hardly consistent with the facts of everyday communication. Indeed, it is highly unlikely that anyone would interpret 'The professor is a snake' literally first, and then proceed to assign a metaphorical meaning to it (unless that person suffered from some kind of neurological dysfunction). Similarly, when a sentence such as, 'The murderer was an animal' is uttered, people will interpret it instinctively as a metaphorical statement, unless they are told that the 'animal' in question is a real animal (a tiger or a bear, perhaps).

Like Aristotle before them (who, incidentally, coined the term *metaphor*), Lakoff and Johnson classify human concepts into concrete and abstract (§1.3). But these two scholars then add a remarkable twist to this fundamental dichotomy: they claim that the two are linked by means of metaphor. In fact, abstract concepts cannot exist in the absolute; they are conceptualized systematically by association with concrete ones that somehow seem to exemplify them. This can be called the 'delivery' of an abstract concept. Thus, 'The professor is a snake' is really a token of an associative mental formula – human personality = animal behaviours – that links an abstract concept (human personality) to the concrete traits we perceive in animals. Utterances of this type – 'John is a gorilla,' 'Mary is a snail,' and so on – are not, therefore, isolated examples of poetic fancy. Rather, they are specific instantiations, or *linguistic metaphors*, of the above mental formula – a formula that Lakoff and Johnson call a *conceptual metaphor*:

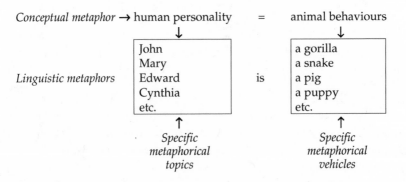

Each of the two parts of the conceptual metaphor is called a *domain* – human personality is the *target domain* because it is the abstract concept (the 'target' of the conceptual metaphor); and animal behaviours is the *source domain* because it represents the concrete concepts that deliver the metaphor (the 'source' of the metaphorical concept). With this framework, it is an easy task to identify the conceptual metaphors that unconsciously guide common everyday language. Take, for example, linguistic metaphors such as the ones below:

1. Those ideas are *circular*, getting us nowhere.
2. I don't see the *point* of your idea.
3. Her ideas are *central* to the entire discussion.
4. Their ideas are *diametrically* opposite.

The target domain inherent in these is 'ideas' and the source domain is 'geometrical figures/relations.' The conceptual metaphor is, therefore: ideas = geometrical figures/relations. The choice of the latter to deliver the concept of ideas is due, in all likelihood, to the experience of using geometry in mathematics and education to generate ideas and to train the mind to think logically. Unconscious conceptual metaphors like these permeate everyday language. This is why Lakoff and Johnson aptly call them 'metaphors we live by.' Their psychological source is the mental *image schemas* that are produced by our sensory experiences of locations, movements, shapes, substances, and so forth as well as by our experiences of social events and of cultural life in general. These thought mediators, so to speak, allow us to objectify our sensations and experiences with words in systematic ways. As the American biologist Ruth Hubbard (b. 1924) has aptly put it: 'Without words to objectify and categorize our sensations and place them in relation to one another, we cannot evolve a tradition of what is real in the world.'[4]

Lakoff and Johnson identify several basic types of image schemas. One involves associating the sensation of orientation or relative location – up vs down, back vs front, near vs far, and so on – with various abstract concepts such as moods and economic trends. This can be seen in linguistic metaphors such as 'I'm feeling *up* today' and 'Inflation is going *down* at last.' A second type involves familiarity with the physical nature of entities and substances that can be, for example, placed in containers or stored in some fashion. This schema is visible in statements such as 'I'm *full* of memories' and 'Can't you get this *into* your head?' A third type involves the perception of how objects and devices work. This schema underlies utterances such as 'My sense of timing is out of sync' and 'Justice must be balanced.' The relevant research has shown that image schemas shape our perceptions of things and events in the world, leading to the formation of cultural groupthink, which is constructed as layers on layers of conceptual metaphors. Lakoff and Johnson call these layers *idealized cognitive models* (ICMs). To grasp what an ICM is about, consider, again, the target domain of ideas. The following three conceptual metaphors, among many others, are used in English-speaking cultures to deliver this concept:

ideas = food

5. Those ideas left a sour *taste* in my mouth.
6. It's hard to *digest* all those ideas at once.
7. Even though he is a *voracious* reader, he can't *chew* all those ideas at once.
8. That teacher is always *spoonfeeding* her students.

ideas = persons

9. Darwin is the *father* of modern biology.
10. Those medieval ideas continue to *live* on even today.
11. Cognitive linguistics is still in its *infancy*.
12. Maybe we should *resurrect* that ancient idea.
13. She breathed new *life* into that idea.

ideas = fashion

14. That idea went *out of style* several years ago.
15. Those scientists are the *avant garde* of their field.
16. Those revolutionary ideas are no longer *in vogue*.
17. Semiotics has become truly *chic*.
18. That idea is an *old hat*.

There are other ways of delivering this target domain – for example, in terms of buildings ('That idea is a *well-constructed* one'), plants ('Those ideas are starting to bear *fruit*'), commodities ('They did not know how to *package* their ideas'), geometry ('Their ideas are *parallel*'), and seeing ('I can't quite *see* the point of your idea'). The constant juxtaposition of these conceptual formulas in common discourse produces, cumulatively, an ICM of ideas. This can be shown with the following diagram:

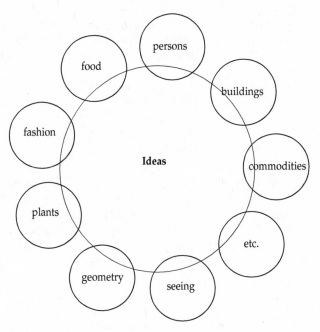

An ICM can thus be described as a 'cognitive clustering' of source domains around a target domain. When the topic of ideas arises in discourse, speakers of English deliver it by navigating conceptually through the various source domains that cluster around it according to need, whim, or situation. For example, the sentence 'I can't see why your ideas aren't catching on, given that they have deep roots and lie on solid ground' has been assembled using three of the above source domains (seeing, plants, and buildings).

ICM theory has many implications, not only for the study of associative structure in itself but also for grasping the nature of cultural groupthink. For example, several of the source domains for the above ICM – food, people, and seeing – are relatively understandable across cultures. That is, people from non-English-speaking cultures could easily figure out what linguistic metaphors based on these domains mean if they were translated or relayed to them. But some source domains are more likely to be culture-specific – for instance, the geometrical figures domain above – and thus beyond smooth cross-cultural comprehension. This suggests that there may be different categories of abstract concepts, some of which are more common in various languages around the world than others. The ideas = food concept, for example, is a basic or root concept because it connects a universal physical process (eating) to an abstraction (thinking) directly. But the ideas = geometrical figures concept reveals a more culture-specific abstraction.

Not all ICMs manifest a clustering structure as it has been described here. This is because another form of cognitive association manifests itself commonly in everyday discourse. This second type inheres in different target domains being delivered by identical source domains. This process can be called *radiation*, since it can be envisioned as a single source domain 'radiating outwards' to deliver different target domains. For example, the plant source domain allows us to conceptualize not only ideas ('That idea has deep *ramifications*'), but also other abstract concepts such as love ('Our love has deep *roots*'), influence ('His influence is *sprouting* all over'), success ('His career has borne great *fruit*'), knowledge ('That discipline has many *branches*'), wisdom ('His wisdom has deep *roots*'), and friendship ('Their friendship is starting to *bud* just now'), among many others. The radiation structure of the above can be shown as follows:

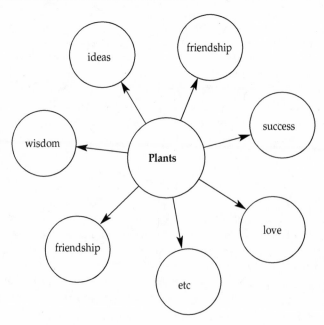

Radiation can be defined as the tendency to envisage some abstract concepts as implicating one another through a specific experiential model or frame of reference (source domain). Radiation, by the way, explains why we talk of seemingly different things, such as wisdom and friendship, with the same metaphorical vehicles. Clustering, on the other hand, explains why we use different metaphorical vehicles to deliver the same concept. In this way, clustering allows people to connect source domains as they talk, for example, about sports: 'The Milwaukee Brewers have a good game plan, but they often fail to implement it; they thus end up constantly in defeat, although one can claim that they have been very unlucky.' This statement makes sense only to those who have acquired the clustering source domains by learning the language involved. This sort of 'domain hopping' is a prevalent feature of discourse. Radiation also has a connective function, but this connectivity is of a different nature. For example, the source domain of the journey is used in English discourse to deliver abstractions such as life, love, and friendship. This is why these topics are sensed to have a connectivity that others do not.

As Lakoff and Johnson pointed out in their 1980 work, associative structure manifests itself in two other rhetorical forms: metonymy (and its counterpart synecdoche) and irony. *Metonymy* is a figure of speech in which an attribute of something is used to stand for the thing itself, as when 'brass' stands for 'military officers.' Synecdoche is a figure of speech in which the word for part of something is used to mean the whole – for example, 'sail' for 'boat.' Thus:

19. She likes to read *Mark Twain* (= the writings of Mark Twain).
20. My mom frowns on *blue jeans* (= the wearing of blue jeans).
21. The *automobile* is destroying us (= the collection of automobiles).
22. I've got a new *set of wheels* (= car).
23. We need *new blood* in this organization (= new people).

In the case of (19), the author's name stands for his writings; in (20) a particular type of garment represents a lifestyle or mode of living; in (21) it is an object that stands for a lifestyle and mode of living; in (22) a part of an object stands for the entire object; and in (23) a vital component of human physical life represents humans themselves. Parallel with the notion of *conceptual metaphor*, the term *conceptual metonym* can be used to refer to such thought formulas. For example, the use of the face as a source domain for personality produces the conceptual metonym 'the face = the person.' This manifests itself commonly in expressions such as the following:

24. He's just another pretty *face*.
25. There are an awful lot of *faces* in the audience.
26. We need some new *faces* around here.
27. You can read his thoughts on his *face*.

Irony involves using words to convey a meaning contrary to their literal sense – for instance, 'I love being tortured' uttered by someone writhing in pain. It is, more formally, a strategy whereby a concept is delivered through association with its opposite, its antithesis, or its antonym. Irony creates a discrepancy between appearance and reality, thus engendering a kind of 'meaning tension by contrast.' It is especially productive in satirical, parodist, and other kinds of captious language. Cultures throughout the world develop their own forms of ironic language. This is why ironic texts are not easily translated from one language to another.

The theory of language laid out in *Metaphors We Live By* has led to extensive research on associative structure generally, and to the development of notions and discoveries such as those discussed above. However, for the sake of historical accuracy it should be noted that *conceptual metaphor theory*, as it is now called, is rooted in the ideas of the literary critic I.A. Richards (1893–1979), who in 1936 suggested that metaphor arises from an association of concepts rather than of single words; this opened the way a little later for the serious scientific investigation of metaphor.[5] A pivotal 1955 study by the gestalt psychologist Solomon Asch subsequently showed that metaphors of sensation in several phylogenetically unrelated languages were based on the same sensory source domains (warm, cold, heavy, etc.), although they varied as to their application to a target domain.[6] For example, he found that 'hot' stood for 'rage' in Hebrew, 'enthusiasm' in Chinese, 'sexual arousal' in Thai, and 'energy' in Hausa. Investigations of these sorts of verbal phenomena proliferated in the 1970s and 1980s. By the early 1990s there was little doubt in the minds of many linguists and semioticians that associative structure in language mirrors the workings of human abstract thinking.

Associative structure also manifests itself in all kinds of verbal and non-verbal sign systems. Consider, again, the conceptual formula human personality = animal behaviours discussed above. In our own culture, we use the names of animals for sports teams (*Chicago Bears, Detroit Tigers, Toronto Blue Jays, Denver Broncos,* etc.), so as to impart character to the team in terms of animal qualities; we utilize cartoon characters *(Bugs Bunny, Daffy Duck,* etc.) to represent human personality types; we tell our children animal stories in order to impart morals to them; and so on and so forth. The gods of many early cultures were conceived as animal figures: Egyptian gods had animal heads; the principal god of the Hindus is Ganesha the elephant; the godhead of the Aztecs was the green-plumed serpent Quetzalcoatl; and so on. Animals are used in astrology to symbolize human character and to predict destiny in tandem with the movement of celestial objects. We may not believe in astrology; nevertheless, we keep an open mind about it, as evidenced by the ubiquity of horoscopes in today's media. Animal metaphors also constitute the central idea behind *totemism,* an Ojibway word. Totems are spiritual entities represented by animal species. A particular totem symbolizes a specific clan. Two people who share the same totem cannot marry. Often, an individual who has a totem – a personal guardian spirit – is forbidden ever to eat the meat of the animal that represents that totem.

This kind of associative semiosis occurs across all kinds of social domains. As one other example, consider our common romance and courtship rituals. In large part these are grounded on a 'love = sweetness' conceptual metaphor ('She's my sweetheart'; 'I love my honey'; etc.). For example, sweets are given to a loved one on Valentine's Day, and matrimonial love is ritualized at a wedding ceremony by the eating of a cake. Similar manifestations are found throughout the world. Among the Chagga, a Bantu society of Tanzania, the male in courtship situations is portrayed as an *eater* and the female as his *sweet food,* as can be detected in expressions that translate as 'Does she taste sweet?' and 'She tastes sweet as sugar honey.'[7]

3.4 Structural Economy

There is an aspect of cyberspace communication and of text-messaging devices that is of particular interest to the study of structure: seemingly in contrast to the traditional forms of writing, such communication is characterized by the use (or abuse, some might say) of all kinds of abbreviations and condensed forms. To the semiotician, this ostensibly new type of written language is really nothing more than a contemporary manifestation of a basic tendency that results from constant sign use – that is, the tendency to reduce the physical form of signs. *Structural economy*, as it might be called, is an inbuilt propensity of human semiotic systems. For example, the English spoken and written today is structurally much more economical than Old English, which had, for example, a full-fledged case system that has virtually disappeared from modern English. So too, the case system of Latin no longer exists in its modern-day descendants (Italian, French, Spanish, etc.). However, such systems are found in German and Norse-based languages. In both languages, sentence length has been greatly reduced by such elimination. The elimination occurred initially because grammatically significant endings of words were not pronounced or written; this led eventually to the abbreviation of words and the consequent elimination of the grammatical categories that their endings marked, bringing about a more general change in overall grammatical structure. The features evident today in text messages – *U2* (you too), *How R U* (How are you?), *b4* (before), *f2f* (face-to-face) *gr8* (great), *g2g* (gotta go), *ezy* (easy), *iluvu* (I love you), *ruok* (Are you OK?) – display an analogous tendency to reduce the length of sentences and other linguistic forms by abbreviating words and using 'letter words' or 'number words' in place of whole words (*U* for *you*, *R* for *are*, *2* for *to*, etc.).

Reduction often correlates with frequency. In other words, the more frequently a form or category is used, the more likely it is that it will be replaced by a shorter equivalent. Structural economy can be seen to undergird common abbreviations and acronyms such as *ad* (advertisement), *photo* (photograph), *NATO* (North Atlantic Treaty Organization), *laser* (light amplification by stimulated emission of radiation), *VCR* (videocassette recorder), *it's* (it is), *UN* (United Nations), *CD* (compact disc), and so on. These save effort and space, and this is why they are used in tables, in technical and scientific materials, and in indexes, footnotes, and bibliographies. Incidentally, reductions have been found on the earliest known tombs, monuments, and coins.

Psychologically, manifestations of structural economy such as those described briefly above suggest the presence of a *principle of least effort* (PLE) in human semiotic and communication behaviours, which can be defined simply as the propensity to reduce the physical structure of signs and sign systems so as to minimize effort in their use and to maximize communication time. The PLE came to the forefront in the 1930s and 1940s when the Harvard linguist George Kingsley Zipf (1902–50) published a series of key studies showing that the most frequently used words in written texts (newspaper articles, novels, etc.) – *a, the, and*, and so on – were also the shortest in length (in terms of the number of alphabet characters that constituted them). The higher the frequency of a word, the more likely it is, Zipf concluded, to show an economy of form (fewer letters, fewer syllables, etc.). More technically, Zipf found an inverse correlation between the length of a specific word (in number of phonemes) and its rank order in the language (in terms of its frequency of occurrence in texts of all kinds). The higher the rank order of a word (the more frequent it was in actual usage), the more it tended to be 'shorter.' Articles, conjunctions, and other such forms, which have a high rank order, are typically monosyllabic, consisting of one to three phonemes.

To grasp the essence of 'Zipf's Law,' as Zipf's discovery came to be called, all one has to do is take the words in a substantial corpus of text, such as an issue of the *New York Times*, and count the number of times each word in it appears. In this endeavour, variants of the same basic word count as separate tokens of that word – for example, *play, played,* and *playing* all count as three manifestations of the same word. If one were then to plot the frequencies of the words on a histogram and sort them by rank, with the most frequently appearing words first, it would be found that the curve approaches a straight line with a slope of –1. The exact same type of result emerges from counting words in textbooks, recipe collections, speeches, novels, and the like. The larger the corpus, the more the curve tends towards this slope. In effect, it would seem to be a fact of language structure that word magnitude tends, on the whole, to stand in an inverse relationship to rank order – the more frequent the word, the shorter it tends to be. Using data from widely divergent languages, Zipf found, moreover, that this was true of any language and that the principle applied not only to words but also to grammatical systems, Chinese characters, and the babbling of babies.

Faced with such statistical regularity, Zipf came to the obvious conclusion that there is an inbuilt tendency in language towards the compression of frequently used forms. This finding stands undisputed to this day. More controversial, however, was Zipf's subsequent reflection that form reduction reflects a universal psychological tendency – the PLE. Many have rejected the PLE, suggesting that Zipfian curves are simple consequences of his particular method of regarding a message source as a random process; it follows that those curves are predictable consequence of probability, not psychology. But many others have accepted the PLE as a general psychological framework for explaining everyday phenomena such as abbreviation and acronymy in language.

For the sake of historical accuracy, it should be mentioned that some of Zipf's ideas were prefigured by various scientists in the nineteenth century. For example, in 1881 the American astronomer Simon Newcomb (1835–1909) found that if the digits used for a task are not entirely random, but somehow socially or naturally based, the distribution of the first digit is not uniform – 1 tends to be the first digit in about 30 per cent of cases, 2 comes up in about 18 per cent of cases, 3 in 12 per cent, 4 in 9 per cent, 5 in 8 per cent, and so on. Newcomb came to this discovery after he noticed that the first pages of books of logarithms were soiled much more than the remaining pages. In 1938 the physicist Frank Benford investigated listings of data and found a pattern similar to the one uncovered by Newcomb in income tax and population figures, as well as in the distribution of street addresses of people listed in phone books. Zipf's main contribution was to show empirically that patterns of this type manifest themselves regularly and 'blindly' in all kinds of human representational efforts, especially in language. Shortly after Zipf's ideas were published, the mathematician Benoit Mandelbrot (b. 1924) – who developed the modern-day branch of mathematics known as fractal geometry – became fascinated by them, detecting in them an indirect confirmation of what is called a 'scaling' law in biology. Mandelbrot made significant mathematical modifications to Zipf's original law – modifications that are used to this day to study structural economy phenomena in language and other sign systems.[8]

The basic implication to be derived from Zipfian analysis can be reformulated in semiotic terms as the *signifier compression principle* (SCP), which posits that the tendency in semiosis is towards the compression of signifiers, even while the meaning range of signifieds is preserved and in some cases actually expanded. The SCP is in some cases related to time. The longer that words and expressions have been around, for instance, the more likely they are to have been compressed, for the simple reason that they are used more frequently. However, this is not always the case; often, simple convenience is the factor leading to compression. The abbreviation *PC* = *personal computer* was compressed almost the instant it entered into currency. The reason here is that PC refers to something that is in constant use. Simply put, compression is the outcome of the tendency to reduce effort, either because of usage over time or because of immediacy of utilization.

In an interesting book titled *The Cognitive Style of PowerPoint*, Edward R. Tufte provides an interesting corroboration of the SCP and its effect on how we deal with meaning.[9] He suggests that software systems such as PowerPoint are changing how we conceive of and present information, since they equate techniques such as bulleting with clear thinking, thereby emphasizing presentation over content; yet at the same time, those systems do not in any way affect the nature of that content – in fact, they are generating new ways of understanding subject matter.

3.5 Post-Structuralism

The classic notions of structuralism – opposition, the semantic differential, the semiotic square, the signifier–signified relation, and so on – are viewed today more as techniques than as comprehensive theories of meaning in themselves, or as elements in such theories. They provide different angles from which to observe meaning in action, so to speak. This does not mean that they do not have implications for understanding what meaning is in a philosophical sense and why we seek it constantly. Indeed, one of the implicit premises of structuralism is (and has always been) that the structures of human semiosis mirror the structures of perception and, ultimately, reality (as understood in a human sense). Oppositions such as *good* vs *evil* are encoded in all kinds of structural systems and forms, from the words that objectify them to the myths that explicate them, because they seem to mirror a dichotomy felt universally by human beings – a dichotomy that finds its way into other linguistic oppositions such as *order* vs *chaos* and *God* vs *the devil*. We will return to the relation between human structures and reality in §6.4.

In the mid-1950s a movement emerged within semiotics known as *post-structuralism*, associated primarily with the French philosophers Michel Foucault (1926–84) and Jacques Derrida (1930–2004), that refuted some of the classic notions of structuralism. A throwback to medieval nominalism and Romantic nihilism (§1.2), the central idea that set off this movement was that signs do not encode reality, but rather construct it. According to Derrida, all sign systems are self-referential – that is, signs refer to other signs, which refer to still other signs, and so on ad infinitum. Thus, what appears stable and logical turns out to be illogical and paradoxical. This is especially (and paradoxically) so in the sciences, which are nothing but products of linguistic conventions. Many semioticians have severely criticized this radical stance of post-structuralism for ignoring veritable discoveries made by the sciences. Nevertheless, post-structuralism had a profound impact on many different fields of knowledge (not just semiotics), including the sciences; this reflects two broader twentieth-century intellectual trends known as absurdism and existentialism. The former holds that human beings exist in a meaningless, irrational universe and that any search for a teleological order by them will bring them into direct conflict with this universe; the latter views human existence as unexplainable and emphasizes the isolation of the individual's experience in a hostile or indifferent universe. In the words of Czech playwright Václav Havel (b. 1936), all such movements point to 'an absence of meaning' in the universe.[10]

So what do post-structuralists analyse, and how does post-structuralism differ from traditional semiotic practice? From a number of perspectives, post-structuralism is really nothing more than structuralism expanded to include a few diverse ideas. Derrida, above anyone else, became fixated with logocentrism – the view that all human knowledge is constructed by linguistic categories – arguing that this very same logocentrism characterized semiotic practices themselves, rendering them virtually useless. Derrida maintained that linguistic forms encode 'ideologies,' not 'reality.' And because written language is the fundamental condition of knowledge-producing enterprises such as science and philosophy, these end up reflecting nothing more than the linguistic categories used to articulate them. Like Derrida, post-structuralists generally critique notions such as truth and logic, given that in no system of knowledge (including the physical sciences) have we ever been able to develop a universal system of representation that does not involve subjectivity and the interpretations of those individuals who have devised the system. As the English novelist George Eliot (1819–80) aptly observed: 'All meanings, we know, depend on the key of interpretation.'[11] For the post-structuralists, signifiers are *empty* structures, devoid of true meaning, and thus can stand on their own (without signifieds) for virtually anything. As the French psychoanalyst Jacques Lacan (1901–81) put it, a signifier separated from its signified shows how our notions of meaning 'slide' into absurdity.

But even before the advent of post-structuralism, semiotics was undergoing a serious self-examination and re-evaluation. By the 1920s, Roman Jakobson (§1.2) and N.S. Trubetskoy (1890–1938) were probing the 'relativity' of language structures in light of their social and psychological functions. Basing their ideas in part on the work of German psychologist Karl Bühler (1879–1963), the Prague School linguists, as they came to be called, posited three main functions of language: the cognitive, the expressive, and the conative (or instrumental). The cognitive function refers to the employment of language to transmit factual information; the expressive to the fact that language allows the speaker (or writer) to convey mood or attitude; and the conative to the use of language to influence the individuals being addressed or to bring about some practical effect via communication. A number of scholars working in the Prague School tradition have suggested that in many languages these three functions correlate, at least in part, with grammatical categories. In effect, grammar does not exist independently of cognition and culture. Another key principle of the Prague School tradition is that language has a poetic basis – a view that has been largely corroborated by the work on conceptual metaphors and ICMs (§3.3).

Roland Barthes, who remained a structuralist to the end of his life, also saw signification as essentially rhetorical in nature. He posited two levels to sign interpretation: the *linguistic* and the *mythical*.[12] The referent of the former exists empirically, having denotative or referential meaning. For example, the word *lion* refers to 'a large, carnivorous, feline mammal of Africa.' But the instant the word is used in social situations, it invariably triggers a mythical (connotative) reaction – namely, a 'very brave person, generally regarded as fierce or ferocious.' Thus, the meaning of the sign oscillates back and forth between the linguistic (denotative) and mythic (connotative) levels in all kinds of contexts. Barthes was also among the first to reject the notion of empty signifier – albeit with a somewhat ambiguous stance, as the following passage shows:[13]

> The signifier is purely a *relatum*, whose definition cannot be separated from that of the signified. The only difference is that the signifier is a mediator: some matter is necessary to it. But on the one hand it is not sufficient to it, and on the other, in semiology, the signifier can, too, be relayed by a certain matter: that of the word. This materiality of the signifier makes it once more necessary to distinguish clearly *matter* from *substance*: a substance can be immaterial (in the case of the substance of the content); therefore, all one can say is that the substance of the signifier is always material (sounds, objects, images).

Closely associated with post-structuralism, the intellectual movement called *postmodernism* emerged in the early 1970s. The term was coined, actually, by architects to characterize a new style that had emerged to counteract so-called modernism in building design, which by mid-twentieth century had degenerated into sterile and monotonous formulas (e.g., box-like skyscrapers). Architects called for greater individuality, complexity, and eccentricity in design, while also demanding acknowledgment of historical precedent and continuity through the innovative reinterpretation of traditional ornamental symbols and patterns. Shortly after its adoption in architecture, the term *postmodernism* started to catch on more broadly, becoming a shibboleth for absurdism, existentialism, and post-structuralism.

The roots of the postmodern outlook can, however, be traced to the nineteenth century, when British biologist Charles Darwin (1809–82) introduced the theory of *natural selection*, which asserts that each generation of a species improves adaptively over the preceding generations and that this gradual and ongoing process is the source of the evolution of the species as a whole. The loudest and strongest attacks on Darwin's ideas came, understandably, from the religious sphere. And they continue to come from that sphere. Even to suggest that human beings could have evolved through natural processes was to deny that God created humankind and to place humanity on a plane with brute animals. Clearly this was a shock to the religious people of Darwin's time. Darwin's ideas posed a serious challenge to religious belief systems, and they continue to do so. However, Darwinian theory could not be denied, starting with a discovery made, ironically, by an Augustinian monk, Gregor Johann Mendel (1822–84). Mendel cultivated and tested more than 28,000 pea plants. His tedious experiments revealed, for instance, that when tall and dwarf parents of peas are cross-bred, hybrid offspring result that resemble the tall parent; in other words, a medium-height blend does *not* result. To explain this, he conceived of hereditary units, now called *genes*, which he contended were responsible for passing on dominant or recessive characteristics. Then, in 1953, nearly a century after Darwin published *The Origin of Species*, biologists James Watson (b. 1928) and Francis Crick (1916–2004) demonstrated that the genetic fabric of all organisms is composed of two nucleic acids, deoxyribonucleic acid (DNA) and ribonucleic acid (RNA) and that natural selection operates by favouring or suppressing particular genes according to how strongly their protein products contribute to the reproductive success of the organism. Put briefly, Darwin's theory posits that human evolution is a matter of genetic reorganization, not divine will.

By the end of the nineteenth century, the now famous assertion that 'God is dead' made by the German philosopher Friedrich Nietzsche (1844–1900) had acknowledged the intellectual revolution that Darwin had launched. What Nietzsche actually meant, of course, was that the grip which the religious world view had on society had finally become loosened by the facts of evolution. By the middle part of the twentieth century, the critique of all aspects of that world view had started in full earnest. By the 1970s, all traditional assumptions about certainty, identity, and truth were coming under close scrutiny in philosophy and the arts, and even within some religions. The term *postmodern* was applied to characterize this turn of events. For the postmodernist, human history has no beginning or end. Human beings fulfil no particular purpose in being alive. Life is a meaningless collage of actions on a relentless course leading to death and to the return to nothingness. Postmodernism started losing its grip on philosophy and the arts in the early 1990s. Today it is viewed (along with post-structuralism) in semiotics as a momentary flight from the most extreme forms of structuralism. Its main contribution to the expansion of human understanding lies – in my view, at least – in the fact that it has reset the agenda in semiotics generally and thereby forced structuralists to look more closely at some of their theoretical and methodological ideas.

In summary, it is accurate to say that semiotics continues to be a structuralist science, but it is also true that it now has incorporated some of the notions and techniques of post-structuralism and some of the ideas of postmodernism into its modus operandi. One of the most important of these is the technique of separating signifiers from signifieds and, thus, of observing the manifestations of meaning in context, instead of viewing meaning as a fixed relation between the two parts of the sign. Signifiers (forms) are now seen as suggesting meanings rather than encoding them. This has allowed semiotics to broaden the way in which it looks at meaning and knowledge generally. In the end, the post-structuralist movement was, arguably, nothing more than a reaction to Saussureanism in its most radical forms. It was (and still is) of little or no interest to semioticians, who work primarily within the framework of the Peircean sign, which emphasizes the interpretive component in semiosis (§1.4).

3.6 Further Reading and Online Resources

Further Reading

Belsey, C. *Poststructuralism*. Oxford: Oxford University Press, 2002.
Derrida, Jacques. *Of Grammatology*. Trans. G.C. Spivak. Baltimore: Johns Hopkins University Press, 1976.

Dirven, René, and Marina Verspoor. *Cognitive Exploration of Language and Linguistics.* Amsterdam: John Benjamins, 1998.

Foucault, Michel. *The Archeology of Knowledge.* Trans. A.M. Sheridan Smith. New York: Pantheon, 1972.

Gibbs, R.W. *The Poetics of Mind: Figurative Thought, Language, and Understanding.* Cambridge: Cambridge University Press, 1994.

Gottdiener, M. *Postmodern Semiotics: Material Culture and the Forms of Postmodern Life.* London: Blackwell, 1995.

Hassan, I. *The Postmodern Turn: Essays in Postmodern Theory and Culture.* Columbus: Ohio State University Press, 1987.

Hawkes, T. *Structuralism and Semiotics.* Berkeley: University of California Press, 1977.

Jameson, Fredric. *Postmodernism or the Cultural Logic of Late Capitalism.* Durham, NC: Duke University Press, 1991.

Lakoff, George, and Mark Johnson. *Philosophy in Flesh: The Embodied Mind and Its Challenge to Western Thought.* New York: Basic, 1999.

– *Metaphors We Live By.* Chicago: University of Chicago Press, 1980.

Lévi-Strauss, Claude. *Structural Anthropology.* New York: Basic, 1958.

Lyotard, J.-F. *The Postmodern Condition: A Report on Knowledge.* Minneapolis: University of Minnesota Press, 1984.

Norris, C. *Deconstruction: Theory and Practice.* London: Routledge, 1991.

Scholes, Robert. *Semiotics and Interpretation.* New Haven, CT: Yale University Press, 1982.

Zipf, G.K. *Human Behavior and the Principle of Least Effort.* Boston: Addison-Wesley, 1949.

– *Psycho-Biology of Languages.* Boston: Houghton-Mifflin, 1935.

Online Resources

Good online sites for getting further information on the topics discussed in this chapter are the following:

(1) For structuralism: http://www.as.ua.edu/ant/Faculty/murphy/struct.
(2) For post-structuralism: http://www.philosopher.org.uk/poststr.
(3) For postmodernism: http://www.library.auckland.ac.nz/subjects/edu/edupost.
(4) For conceptual metaphor theory: http://www.philosophy.uoregon.edu/metaphor/metaphor.html.
(5) For Zipf's Law: http://www.nist.gov/dads/HTML/zipfslaw.htm.

4 Codes

Form and function are a unity, two sides of one coin. In order to enhance function, appropriate form must exist or be created.

Ida P. Rolf (1896–1979)

4.1 Introduction

In the preface to this book, it was mentioned that Dan Brown's *The Da Vinci Code* became a best-seller not only because it tapped into a timely theme (the victimization of women by religion) but also because it tapped into people's love of mystery stories. The mystery in this case was solved through the use of 'detective semiotics' (called 'symbology' by Brown). The novel is about a puzzling code, called the 'Da Vinci Code,' which the protagonist Robert Langdon – a 'symbologist' – ultimately decodes by interpreting the individual clues to its meaning scattered throughout the plot. The notion of *code* is, to the semiotician, a basic one for explaining how we interpret all kinds of meaningful texts, not just mystery stories.

Codes are found in all domains of human intellectual and social life, from the juridical (e.g., the *legal code*) to the recreational (e.g., *cryptogram codes* and non-existent 'Da Vinci codes'). Codes are systems of signs that people can select and combine in specific ways (according to the nature of the code) to construct messages, carry out actions, enact rituals, and so on, in meaningful ways. Stories, fashion styles, musical compositions, and the like are all code-based productions. In strictly semiotic terms, the rules that characterize codes are (as discussed in the previous chapter) the paradigmatic, syntagmatic, associative, and other formal relations that characterize sign constitution. This chapter looks at the nature of codes and at how they inform the entire network of meanings in a culture.

4.2 What Is a Code?

Consider the English alphabet. What comes after *G*? The answer is, of course, *H*. How do we know this? We know this because we are familiar with the letters of the alphabet and because we have memorized the order in which they are organized. The alphabet is a perfect example of a *code* – a system of signs that are perceptibly distinct and that can be combined in specific ways to make words. Like the actual signs that comprise them, codes can be natural or conventional. As discussed earlier (§1.2 and §2.3), the former are produced by nature (e.g., the *genetic code*), and the latter are produced by culture-specific events, practices, traditions, and so on – for example, the order in which our alphabet letters are sequenced is the result of the Ancient Greek practice of letting letters stand for numbers (A = 1, B = 2, etc.).

Take cryptography as another case in point. This is defined as the science of constructing 'concealed messages' using symbolic strategies and techniques intended to be intelligible only to those possessing the key, or method, of deciphering the messages. These include transposing letters (*rwod* for *word*), substituting symbols for the original letters (*2834* for *word*, in which *w* = 2, *o* = 8, *r* = 3, *d* = 4), and using a combination of different symbols and techniques. In transposition codes, the message is usually written, without word divisions, in rows of letters arranged in a rectangular block. The letters are then transposed in a prearranged order such as by vertical columns, diagonals, or spirals, or by more complicated systems. In substitution codes, a particular letter or symbol is substituted for each letter of the words in a message. The letters are left in their normal order, usually with normal word divisions. In multiple substitution codes, a keyword or number is employed. The first letter might be given the numerical value of the first letter of the keyword; the second, similarly, the second letter of the keyword; and so on. In more complicated systems, the keyword may indicate which of a series of symbols hides each letter of the message.

As an example of a simple substitution cipher, consider the following combination of letters:

JGNNQ

We know that each letter represents another letter of the alphabet and that the sequence stands for an actual word. With a bit of trial and error, it can be seen that the actual English word is *Hello*. The code consists in replacing each letter of the alphabet with the second letter after it in the normal sequence: H = J, E = G, L = N (twice), and O = Q. This example is instructive in that it shows two things about codes in general: (1) to understand any message we must know the code with which it was constructed; and (2) a message can be put together with several codes, independently or in combination. To understand a simple handshake as indicating a greeting, we must understand the haptic code with which it is constructed (§2.3) as well as grasp the fact that it involves not only tactility but also the language code ('Hello,' 'Nice to meet you,' etc.).

Conventional codes govern all aspects of human intellectual and social life. As just mentioned, in order to make contact with someone successfully we must know the appropriate haptic and language codes. These provide the forms (words, expressions, which hands are involved, the length of the shaking, and so on) and the rules for combining them that make interaction possible in the first place. Similarly, music, painting, and other kinds of codes provide and specify the ways in which tones, harmonies, colours, figures, and the like can be selected and combined to create texts of various kinds, such as symphonies and portraits. These 'ways' are not invented on the spot, so to speak. They are products of historical processes. Pop music, for instance, is based on the same harmonic code that baroque musicians established more than 250 years ago in Europe. And those musicians came to their own harmonic practices on the basis of previous styles in music.

Three general features define codes. The first one can be called *representationality*. This implies that the signs and the rules for combining them in codes can be used to stand for – *represent* – something. The end result of representation is a text of some kind that contains (or is assumed to contain) a message. The second one can be called *interpretability*. This implies that messages can be understood successfully only by someone who is familiar with the signs and rules of the codes used to construct them. The third is *contextualization*. This implies that message interpretation is affected by the context in which it occurs. In communication science, representationality is known as *encoding*, and both interpretability and contextualization as *decoding*. For instance, the social messages conveyed by clothing items are the result of implicit dress codes that bear socially relevant meanings in specific contexts. The items that constitute the business suit 'encode' or 'represent' vastly different meanings and produce enormously different 'interpretations' or 'decodings' than those which make up the punk-rocker clothing style. When people put these items on their bodies, in specific social contexts, they are producing specific types of messages. This topic will be discussed further in the final chapter (§7.2).

Contextualization is the reason why interpretation is not an open-ended process. This term is used often throughout the relevant semiotic literature. It can be defined as the environment, situation, or process – physical, psychological, or social – that governs interpretation (decoding). Consider a discarded and damaged beer can. If one were to come across this object on a sidewalk on a city street, the tendency would be, no doubt, to interpret it as a piece of garbage or rubbish. But if one saw the very same object on a pedestal, displayed in an art gallery, 'signed' by some artist, and given a title such as 'Waste,' then one would be inclined to interpret it in a vastly different way – as a work of art symbolizing a throwaway or materialistic society. Clearly, the can's physical context of occurrence – its location on a sidewalk vs its display in an art gallery – will determine how it will be interpreted. The art gallery is, in effect, a social code. Anything that is put on display within it is assumed to be art. Not possessing knowledge of this code, children would hardly be inclined to interpret the beer can as an art form; they would see it as a beer can, no matter where it is located. As children grow up and become familiar with the code, they will also become accustomed to interpreting objects in galleries, such as beer cans, differently.

As products of history and tradition, conventional codes bear evidence of the contextualized experiences of communities. Take the language code as an example. The Inuit language, for example, has specialized terms for the animal we call a *seal* in English – one is the general term for 'seal'; another renders the idea of 'seal basking in the sun'; a third, 'seal floating on a piece of ice.' English uses only the word *seal* to refer to the animal in all such contexts. This is so because English-speaking communities have not lived (in the past) in places where seals play as crucial a role for survival as they do (to this day) in Inuit life. The specialized terms for seals that were created by Inuit communities are the result of different contextualized experiences from those of English-speaking communities. But this is not to imply that English speakers cannot understand the concepts captured by the Inuit words and the rationale behind them. The paraphrases used above to convey the various meanings of the terms show that there are always ways in which the resources of any language can be used to communicate meanings cross-culturally. Clearly, language codes, social life, and knowledge are interdependent. Put another way, the identification, naming, and grouping of the 'objects of reality' is a contextualized semiotic process. However, once the 'objects' have been encoded by language (or some other code) they are perceived as 'necessary' or 'natural' discoveries of reality, not just as convenient signs.

The relation between knowledge and signs has been debated since antiquity. St Augustine (§1.2), for example, suggested that language gives form to knowledge: 'But how is it that a word which is not yet formed in the vision of the thought? How will it be like the knowledge of which it is born, if it has not the form of that knowledge, and is only now called a word because it can have it?'[1] Similarly, in his *Ars Logica* and *Tractatus de Signis*, Poinsot (§1.2) saw words as having 'cognitive power' because they produce observable effects on their users. First, there is a *productive* effect or 'the power itself which elicits an act of knowledge.'[2] Second, there is an *objective* effect 'toward which a cognition tends, as when I see a stone or a man.'[3] Third, there is a *formal* effect, which 'is the awareness itself whereby a power is rendered cognizant, as the sight itself of the stone or of the man.'[4] Fourth, there is an *instrumental* effect, which 'is the means by which the object is represented to the power, as a picture of Caesar represents Caesar.'[5] Saussure, too, claimed that the 'real world' cannot be known directly by the human mind, since that very world is filtered by language. This view was echoed by Saussurean scholars throughout the twentieth century. The French linguist Émile Benveniste (1902–76), for instance, emphasized that words are constructed in the mind purely as a result of their usage in daily life, and the Danish linguist Louis Hjelmslev (§1.3) maintained that words encoded those meanings which a society required of them.

As another example of the relation between knowledge and codes, consider common *maps*. A map is a visual text designed to represent real-world places in specific ways. But maps are hardly neutral in the way they actually carry out representation. Each map is the result of a pre-existing code. A basic feature of the code is the demarcation line. By drawing demarcation lines around territories, maps end up reifying those very territories on various levels of interpretation. A map of the world, for example, shows not only the physical structure of territories, but also the historical status of nationhood through the demarcation technique. And like any other code-based system of representation, map-making is adaptive, changing in tandem with the political and historical events that alter nationhood.

The earliest existing maps were made by the Babylonians about 2300 BCE. They were used mainly for land surveys and for purposes of taxation. The first map to represent the known world is believed to have been made in the sixth century BCE by the Greek philosopher Anaximander (611–547 BCE). One of the most famous maps of classical times was drawn by the Greek geographer Eratosthenes around 200 BCE. It represented the known world from England to Africa to India and was the first to have transverse parallel lines to show equal latitudes. After the fall of the Roman Empire, European map making all but ceased. Arab sailors, however, made highly accurate terra firma charts during this same period. In the fifteenth century, editions of the maps of the Greek mathematician and astronomer Ptolemy were printed in Europe; for the next several hundred years these exerted great influence on European cartographers. In 1568 the Flemish geographer Gerardus Mercator (1512–94) devised the technique of map projection that bears his name. In 1570 the Flemish map maker Abraham Ortelius published the first modern atlas. It contained seventy maps. By the eighteenth century, the scientific principles of map making were well established and a number of European countries were undertaking detailed national cartographic projects, presumably to define themselves on paper, so to speak. During the twentieth century, map making underwent a series of major technical innovations. Aerial photography was developed first, satellite surveying a little later. Satellite photographs can furnish a wealth of accurate information about various features of the earth's surface, enabling its representation with virtually no distortion.

As representations of terra firma, maps have navigational and exploratory functions. In the same way that the sciences of geometry and trigonometry have allowed human beings to solve engineering problems since ancient times, the science of cartography has allowed travellers and explorers to solve navigation and exploration problems with amazing efficiency. This suggests that exploration is a sign-based process. Exploration involves determining position and direction. Position is a point on the earth's surface that can be identified in terms of a grid or coordinate system. Direction is the position of one point relative to another within the system. The shortest distance between two points is a straight line, and since any line on the plane is a hypotenuse, its length can be determined easily by the Pythagorean theorem. Maps have allowed navigators to fix points and determine distances to regions of the earth's surface. Explorers setting out on a journey in the past may not have known what they would encounter along the way, nor would they have known in advance whether they would reach a land mass or a body of water. But they still took the journey confidently, because their maps allowed them to predict where they would end up, more or less, on terra firma (or at least so they thought). Codes are perceived as representing reality, until proven otherwise.

4.3 Opposition and Markedness

As sign systems, codes are characterized by opposition (§3.2). For example, binary opposition operates across a vast array of codes – in the language code, it operates at the level of sound (e.g., *cat* vs *rat)*; in the musical code, at the level of tones and harmonies (e.g., *major* vs *minor)*; in the mythical code, at the historical–conceptual level (e.g., *good* vs *evil*). On the other hand, square oppositions (e.g., *rich* vs *not rich* vs *poor* vs *not* poor) seem to be operative in verbal and logic codes, such as language and narrative.

For the sake of historical accuracy, it should be mentioned that the concept of opposition is hardly an invention of semioticians. It is an ancient notion. Aristotle, for instance, developed his philosophical system on the basis of a set of existential oppositions: Unity vs Multiplicity, Being vs Non-Being, and others. Opposition is a widespread notion that has surfaced in the philosophical, religious, and other writings of cultures around the world. The following oppositions seem to be universal – that is, they are found in the representational traditions of societies around the world:

Masculine	vs	Feminine
Light	vs	Dark
Good	vs	Evil
Self	vs	Other
Subject	vs	Object
Sacred	vs	Profane
Body	vs	Mind
Nature	vs	History
Positive	vs	Negative
Heaven	vs	Hell	(*continued*)

Beginning   vs   End
Love   vs   Hate
Pleasure   vs   Pain
Existence   vs   Nothingness
Left   vs   Right

As Saussure aptly observed, oppositions seem to undergird human meaning systems.[6] As an example of how a single binary opposition is encoded in various systems, consider the Left vs Right one. This is derived, obviously, from the fact that we have a left hand (and foot, leg, ear, and eye) and a right one. Here are a few of the ways in which this physically based opposition is encoded:

- It intersects with other oppositions – Right is associated with Good, Light, and Left with Evil, Dark, etc. The English word *sinister* derives from the Latin *sinistra*, 'on the left, unlucky,' linking left-handedness with connotations of evil and misfortune.
- In the fresco of Michelangelo's *Last Judgment* on the ceiling of the Sistine Chapel, Christ is depicted as condemning Evil sinners to Hell with his left hand but permitting passage to Heaven for Good people with a blessing of his right hand.
- The word *right* is used commonly in English-speaking societies (and others) to convey concepts of 'correctness,' 'truth,' and 'justice.' In the United States, the Bill of Rights is a legal document that lays out the *rights* to which each person is entitled. Canada has a similar document called the Charter of Rights and Freedoms.
- A *righteous* person is defined as someone moral, and thus without guilt or sin.
- A *right-hand man* is someone with considerable power and authority.
- English has adopted the French word *gauche*, which literally means 'left,' to describe someone who lacks social polish or who is tactless.
- Offering a handshake, saluting, or taking an oath with the left hand is considered improper and wrong.

The list of manifestations of the Right vs Left opposition is a huge one. The plausible reason why we have come to assign positive connotations to the Right member of the opposition and negative connotations to the Left one probably stems from the fact that most human beings use the right hand to carry out routine tasks. It is estimated that only about 10 per cent of the population is left-handed. As a consequence, the right hand is perceived to be the default form of human handedness. This form is called, more precisely, the *unmarked* form in semiotic theory; the other one is called the *marked* form. However, it is to be noted that *markedness* is hardly a phenomenon of nature. Nature makes no social distinctions between right-handed and left-handed individuals; people do. As can be seen by examining the opposition sets above, determining which member of a pair is the unmarked form and which one the marked is more a matter of tradition and history than it is of anything else. Good, for example, has always been assumed to be the default form of human behaviour in many societies, while Evil has always been perceived to be its antagonistic counterpart. Good is unmarked (the default) and Evil is marked (the deviation).

Markedness has implications for studying how people perceive reality. Take, for instance, languages that represent male and female human beings in grammatically and lexically distinct ways, thus encoding the Masculine vs Feminine opposition in a concrete manner. In English, the masculine gender was once considered to be the unmarked one. This is why terms like *chairman, spokesman,* and the like were used in the not too distant past to suggest that the male gender is the default one. Feminist critics maintained (correctly) that this was so because English grammar reflected the perspective of those at the centre of the society – the men. In the recent past (and even to some extent today) people would say that a woman *married into a man's family.* Similarly, at wedding ceremonies clerics would ordinarily use the expression *I pronounce you man and wife,* and never *I pronounce you man and woman* or *I pronounce you wife and husband.* Such language portrayed women as subjugated to men. But that was not all. English also tended to depict women as being 'atypical' in certain social roles. Expressions such as *lady atheist* or *female doctor,* for example, implied that atheists and doctors are not typically female. Such expressions have been virtually eradicated from conversation; nevertheless, they show how markedness provides an insight into social behaviour and structure.

By the way, in some societies the reverse situation is true. In the Iroquois language, the feminine gender is the default (unmarked) one, whereas masculine forms are marked by a special prefix. This grammatical system has resulted, undoubtedly, from the fact that the Iroquois society is matrilineal – traditionally, women hold the land, pass it on to their heirs in the female line, are responsible for agricultural production, control the wealth, arrange marriages, and so on. The Iroquois language reflects this contextualized reality by assigning greater status to those at the centre of that society – in this case, the women. In effect, this example further emphasizes the importance of markedness, and more generally, of opposition, in unravelling the reasons behind certain social behaviours and perceptions. In sum, the oppositions encoded in language and other semiotic systems are culture-specific ways of reacting to contextualized realities.

4.4 Types of Codes

There are many codes, and each has specific functions. In this section the discussion will be limited to a brief consideration of four major types of codes – social, mythic, knowledge, and narrative. The salient feature of each code is that it contains elements that signify something when they are organized or utilized in some way. They may not look like signs, but they are in the abstract sense of the word *semeion* (something standing for something else in some way).

Social codes underlie social communication and interaction. Consider, as a case in point, the zones that people maintain between one another during greeting rituals. Each zone is, in fact, a sign of social proximity. The interpretation of zones unfolds according to a general principle – namely, the closer people stand to one another, the more they are perceived as being on familiar or intimate terms. In the 1950s, the anthropologist Edward T. Hall started measuring these zones.[7] He found that a distance of under six inches is perceived as an intimate zone reserved for love making, comforting, and protecting. A six to eighteen inch zone is where family members and close friends interact in routine situations. Touch is frequent in both these zones. An eighteen-inch to four-foot zone is the minimum comfortable space that non-touching individuals tend to maintain. In the close phase (eighteen to thirty inches) one individual can grasp the other by extending the arms. The far phase (thirty to forty-eight inches) is anywhere from one arm's length to the minimum distance in which two individuals can touch hands. Beyond this distance the two must move towards each other in order to make contact (e.g., to shake hands). A four to twelve foot zone is perceived as non-involving and non-threatening by most individuals. The close phase (four to seven feet) is typical of impersonal transactions and casual social gatherings. Formal social discourse and transactions are characteristic of the far phase (seven to twelve feet). Finally, the twelve feet and beyond zone constitutes the most formalized zone. People tend to keep at this distance from important public figures. Discourse at this distance tends to be highly structured and formalized (lectures, speeches, etc.). In sum, the zones maintained by people during interaction are governed by a spatially based social code that tells people how to interpret physical nearness and farness in emotional and social ways.

Mythic codes abound, whether we realize it or not. Take, for example, the hero code. In the ancient world, a number of real and imaginary figures such as Achilles, Prometheus, and Samson were perceived as 'heroes.' They were signs of personality traits – courage, nobility, strength, sacrifice, and so forth – that were (and continue to be) considered as ideal. The narratives that were composed about them were all based on an implicit 'hero code' that consisted of several salient features – for example, the hero came from another world; he possessed superhuman strength; however, he had a 'flaw' that rendered him vulnerable in certain situations; and so on. This hero code has hardly disappeared from the contemporary world. It surfaces in various guises, from comic book action heroes to more mundane heroes such as detectives and spies (e.g., Sherlock Holmes and James Bond). Like the ancient heroes of myth and legend, these fictitious heroes are strong, superhuman (to varying degrees), have a tragic flaw, and so on. The action hero Superman comes from another world (the planet Krypton); he has superhuman qualities (he can fly, he cannot be killed by human means, etc.); he helps weaker humans and defeats villains; he has a tragic flaw (exposure to the fictitious substance kryptonite takes away his power); and so on. The Superman figure has been grafted directly from the mythic hero code of the ancient world.

Knowledge codes allow for the representation and communication of knowledge of various kinds, from logical, mathematical, scientific, and philosophical to classificatory and legal. A perfect example of a knowledge code is trigonometry. Its elements, known as *functions*, are defined in terms of a given acute angle in a right triangle:

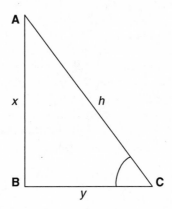

The *sine* (sin) of the angle at **C** is the ratio of the opposite side to the hypotenuse, x/h; the *cosine* (cos) is the ratio of the adjacent side to the hypotenuse, y/h; the *tangent* (tan) of **C** is the ratio of the opposite side to the adjacent side x/y; the *cotangent* (cot) of **C** is the ratio of the adjacent to the opposite side, y/x; the *secant* (sec) of **C** is the ratio of the hypotenuse to the adjacent side, h/y; and the *cosecant* is the ratio of the hypotenuse to the opposite side, h/x. For any angle the numerical values of the trigonometric ratios can be easily approximated by drawing the angle, measuring, and then calculating the ratios. It was the ancient Babylonians who established the measurement of angles in triangles. In the second century BCE the Greek astronomer Hipparchus (c. 190–c. 120 BCE) compiled the first true trigonometric table. What is the function of such a code, one might ask? As it turns out, this simple code can be applied to solve real-world problems. By envisioning an immeasurable distance as one side of a triangle, measuring other sides or angles of the triangle, and applying the appropriate trigonometric ratios, distance can be easily determined. The earliest applications of trigonometry were, in fact, in the fields of navigation, surveying, and astronomy, where the main problem is to determine an inaccessible distance, such as the distance between the earth and the moon or the distance across a large lake.

Take, as a simple example, the following problem:

From a lighthouse, an observer sees a boat at an angle of depression of 43°. If the observer's eyes are 39 metres above the water, how far is the boat from the base of the lighthouse?

Trigonometry makes solving what would otherwise be an intractable problem a simple affair. First, let's draw a diagram that, in its bare outline, can be seen to represent what is known about the situation. Assuming that the lighthouse is standing upright, we can draw it as a straight line, 39 meters in length, above the water. Since we do not know the distance of the boat from the base of the lighthouse, we can represent it with the letter d. By joining the point where the boat is seen at distance d to the observer's eyes on top of the lighthouse, we can draw a triangular model of the scene as follows:

Eye point = Height of the lighthouse

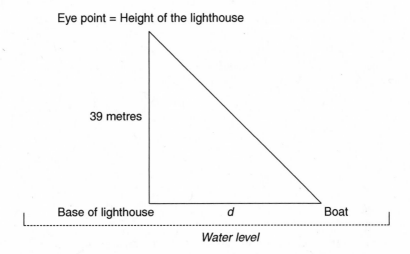

Now, since the angle of depression – the angle measured down from the horizontal to the boat – is given as 43°, we can mark it on the diagram as follows:

Eye point = Height of the lighthouse

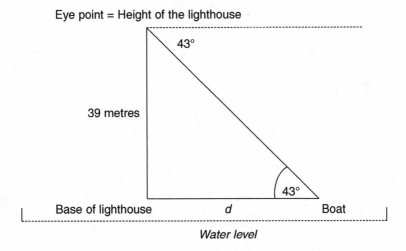

Because the horizontal is parallel to the water – that is, to line d – the angle between d and the hypotenuse is, by a proposition of Euclidean geometry, also 43°. We can now consider the triangle on its own, without reference to the real-world problem it represents. The triangle is a representamen in the Peircean sense of that term. The tan of angle 43° is the ratio $39/d$ (the ratio of the opposite side to the adjacent side). We can now set up an equation as follows, and solve for d, since we know (from the appropriate trigonometric function table) that tan 43° is 0.932515:

$$\tan 43° = 0.932515$$
$$39/d = \tan 43°$$
$$39/d = 0.932515$$
$$d = 39/0.932515$$
$$d = 41.8$$

With this simple representamen we have been able to determine the distance of the boat from the base of the lighthouse as (approximately) 41.8 metres. As this example shows, knowledge codes are truly remarkable. They suggest that only with representations of the world can we come to understand that very world.

A fourth major type of code is known as a *narrative code*. A narrative is a story that is put together to portray reality in a specific way. It is a representation of human events as they are perceived to be related to the passage of time. The 'time frame' may be the past or the future (as in science fiction stories); or it may be an unspecified period of time (*Once upon a time...*), which suggests that the story is about a universal theme. The narrative may be based in fact, as in a newspaper report, or a psychoanalytic session, or it may be fictional, as in a novel, a comic strip, or a film. Needless to say, it is often difficult if not impossible to determine the boundary line between narrative fact and fiction.[8]

Narrative is a primary means of recreation, enjoyment, and education in cultures around the world. Papyri from the IV Egyptian Dynasty indicate that King Cheops (2590–2567 BCE) delighted in hearing fictional stories that his sons told him. The Greek statesman and general Aristides (530?–468? BCE) wrote a collection of what we would now call *short stories* about his hometown, Miletus, to celebrate his countrymen's victory over the Persians at Salamis. The *Golden Ass* of Apuleius (125?–200? AD) in Latin constituted a fictional narration aimed at providing social and moral commentary. By and large, the ancient tales were mainly about the gods and the foibles of human beings. Narratives about common people became popular only in medieval times, after the Italian Giovanni Boccaccio (1313–75) wrote the *Decameron*, a collection of one hundred fictional tales set against the gloomy background of the Black Death – as the bubonic plague that swept through Europe in the fourteenth century was called. The *Decameron* is the first real example of narrative fiction in the modern sense of the word – the telling of stories just for the sake of the telling. To escape an outbreak of the plague, ten friends take refuge in a country villa outside Florence. There they entertain one another over a period of ten days with a series of stories told by each member of the party in turn. Each day's storytelling ends with a *canzone*, a short lyric poem. The *Decameron* is a penetrating analysis of human character.

The scholar who is best known for studying narratives from a semiotic perspective is the late Algirdas Greimas (§1.2). Greimas's main contention was that human beings in different cultures invent remarkably similar stories with virtually the same plots, characters, and settings because they utilize a universal narrative code, which he called an 'actantial grammar.' The 'parts of speech' of this grammar (the characters, settings, etc.) are *actants*. Actually, the notion of actant was already implicit in Vladimir Propp's 1928 analysis of the Russian folktale, in which Propp identified thirty-one actants (although he did not call them that) – the hero, the false hero, the antagonist, the donor, the helper, the dispatcher, and so on.[9] The first to name these *actants* was the French linguist Lucien Tesnière, who defined them as 'beings or things that participate in processes in any form and in any way whatsoever.'[10] Greimas reduced Propp's categories to various fundamental oppositions such as Subject vs Object, Sender vs Receiver, and Helper vs Opponent. These, he suggested, can be applied to all kinds of narratives. Take, for instance, the pop culture *Batman* narrative. The hero in this case is, of course, Batman himself; the helper is his partner Robin; the opponent takes on various characters depending on actual story, from the Riddler to the Penguin; and so on. Also Batman and Robin employ an arsenal of weapons and gadgets in fighting crime, including a Batmobile and Batplane and Batman's all-purpose utility belt. These are also helper actants, although they intersect with other actantial categories.

Discussing how actantial theory has been used in semiotics is beyond the purpose of this text. Suffice it to say that Greimas and his followers extended it to suggest that it had implications for sign theory generally since, after all, signs are fundamentally actants – forms of abstract action that are given concrete expression in discourse, ritual, and the like. Greimas's approach is not accepted universally by semioticians; nevertheless, it posits a number of interesting ideas that do seem to cut across various schools of thought. In my own view, the Propp-Greimas approach has been useful in the semiotic analysis of codes mainly because it has identified certain basic oppositions of the narrative code.

4.5 Codes and Perception

Much of the above discussion has been grounded in an implicit premise – namely, that codes influence how humans come to perceive the world. Is this premise tenable? Recall the earlier discussion of specialized vocabularies (§4.2). These are created by specific communities to encode realities that they perceive to be critical to their communal experiences. They are products of history and tradition and, consequently, mark cognitive differences among communities. Consider colour terminology. Experts estimate that we can distinguish perhaps as many as ten million colors. Names for colours are, thus, far too inexact for us to describe accurately all the colours we actually see – no matter what the language is. If one were to place a finger on any point along the spectrum, there would be only a negligible difference in gradation in the colours immediately adjacent to the finger on either side. Yet a speaker of English describing the spectrum will list the gradations as falling under categories such as *purple, blue, green, yellow, orange, red*, and so on. This is because that speaker has been conditioned by the English language to classify the content of the spectrum in specific ways. There is nothing inherently 'natural' about the English colour scheme; it is a reflex of vocabulary, not of nature. What is a shade in one language is a distinct colour in another.

Put briefly, the type of vocabulary that develops in a specific language is largely a matter of cultural emphasis, need, or tradition. It is a product of historical forces, not natural ones. Consider, as another example, the way in which a device that marks the passage of time is named differentially in English and Italian. In the former language it is called a *watch* if it is portable and worn on the human body (usually on the wrist), but a *clock* if it is to be put in some place – for example, on a table or a wall. The Italian language has not encoded this distinction. The word *orologio* refers to any device for keeping track of time, whether it is worn or carried on the human body or not. The 'referential ranges' of the two vocabularies can be compared using a diagram such as the one below, which shows that the semantic range of *orologio* is equivalent to that of *watch* and *clock*:

Italian	*orologio*	
English	*watch* (portable)	*clock* (non-portable)
Concept	'device for keeping track of time'	

Now, this differential vocabulary pattern does not imply that Italian lacks the linguistic resources for making the same type of distinction that English makes, if needed. Indeed, the phrase *da* + place allows speakers to provide detailed information about the time-keeping device's location:

> *orologio da polso* = 'wrist watch'
> *orologio da tavolo* = 'table clock'
> *orologio da muro* = 'wall clock'
> etc.

Italians do not (or more precisely did not) find it necessary to distinguish between watches and clocks, especially since they can refer to the portability of the device in other ways, if the situation requires them to do so. Speakers of English, on the other hand, refer to the portability distinction as a necessary fact of life, attending to it on a regular basis, as witnessed by the two words in its lexicon. Historically speaking, the word *watch* originated in the 1850s when people started strapping time devices around their wrists. As the psychologist Robert Levine argues, this introduced a fixation with watching time pass that has been encoded into the English language with the *clock* vs *watch* dichotomy.[11]

The idea that language, thought, and culture are interlinked generally falls under the rubric of the Whorfian Hypothesis (WH), named after the American anthropological linguist Benjamin Lee Whorf (§1.5) and sometimes after both him and his teacher Edward Sapir (the Sapir-Whorf Hypothesis). It also goes under the name of the Linguistic Relativity Hypothesis. The WH has been debated extensively, especially within linguistics and psychology. Entering into this interesting debate is well beyond the scope of the present treatment. Suffice it to say here that the WH posits, basically, that languages predispose speakers to attend to certain concepts as being necessary. But, as Whorf himself emphasized, this does not mean that understanding between speakers of different languages is blocked. On the contrary, through translation people are always attempting to understand one another. Moreover, as discussed several times in this chapter, the resources of any language allow its speakers to invent new categories any time they want. All of this is not to deny the fact that words create thoughts and that these become habitualized and thus perceived as necessary. For example, if for some reason we decided to refer to 'adolescent boys between the ages of thirteen and sixteen who wear nose rings,' then by coining an appropriate word, such as *narb*, we would in effect be etching this concept into our minds. When a boy with the stated characteristics came into view, we would immediately recognize him as a narb, thinking of him as exemplifying a distinct class of individuals. When we name something, we are classifying. What we are naming belongs to no class until we place it in one. A plausible framework for studying the implications of the WH, therefore, is to assume that there is a dynamic between codes and perception, with one influencing the other.

The overall philosophical and psychological implications of the WH is that there is a constant interaction between human sign systems and nature – one influences the other. The late Estonian semiotician Jurij Lotman (1922–93) suggested, in fact, that culture be renamed the *semiosphere*. Like the biosphere – the environment or habitat to which a species has become adapted – the semiosphere regulates and shapes perception and cognition. Although they can do little about the biosphere, humans have the ability to reshape the semiosphere any time they want – hence the dynamic that inheres between signs (such as words) and perception. This dynamic is the reason why cultures are both restrictive and liberating. They are restrictive in that they impose on individuals born into them an already fixed system of sign use. This system will largely determine how people come to understand the world around them in terms of the language, music, myths, rituals, technological systems, and other codes that they learn in social context. But cultures are also liberating because, paradoxically, they provide the signifying resources by which individuals can seek new meanings on their own. The many codes to which individuals are exposed in social contexts stimulate creativity. As a result, human beings tend to become restless for new meanings, new ways to represent the world. For this reason, codes are constantly being modified by new generations of artists, scientists, philosophers, and others to meet new demands, new ideas, new challenges.

Leaving aside this knack for creativity for the moment, the fact remains that the semiosphere influences beliefs, attitudes, world views, and sensory perceptions to varying degrees. As a concrete example, consider the following figure, in which two lines of equal length actually appear unequal to the visual perception of most people living in Western societies (and possibly others):

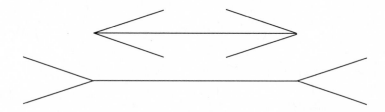

The lower line appears to be longer because of the outward orientation of the arrowheads. In Western art codes, outward means 'away' and thus 'longer,' while 'inward' means 'getting closer.' In other areas of the world, where this outward vs inward opposition is not part of pictorial codes, psychologists have found that people are not duped by the above illusion. Optical illusions provide strong evidence to support the notion that codes mediate perception. The great Swiss psychologist Carl Jung (1875–1961) was fond of recounting how visual perception is intrinsically intertwined with representational practices. During a visit to an island tribal culture that had never been exposed to illustrated magazines, he found that the people of that culture were unable to recognize the photographs in the magazines as visual representations of human beings. To his amazement, he discovered that they perceived them, rather, as smudges on the paper. Jung understood perfectly well, however, that their erroneous interpretation of the photographs was not due to defects of intelligence or eyesight; on the contrary, the tribal members were clear-sighted and highly intelligent. Jung perceptively understood that their primary assumptions were different from his own and from those of individuals living in Western culture, because they had acquired a different system of signs that blocked them from perceiving the pictures as visual signs.

Because humans live in the semiosphere, they are bound to perceive only a small selective part of what constitutes reality. The semiosphere always leaves gaps, offering up only a portion of what is potentially knowable in the world. Indeed, humans are constantly inventing new forms (signs, texts, codes) to fill in the gaps. Gap filling is in fact a human impulse that manifests itself from early childhood on. This is why children make up 'nonsense' words. The great British author of children's books Lewis Carroll (1832–98) invented his own nonsense language in the poem *Jabberwocky*, in order to show that the English language as constituted does not tell all there is to tell about reality. Coining words such as *brillig, slithy, tove, wabe*, and others (*Through the Looking Glass*, 1871), Carroll showed that it is an easy thing to make up legitimate verbal signifiers that seem to beg for equally legitimate meanings:

brillig = 'the time of broiling dinner,' 'the close of the afternoon'
slithy = 'smooth and active'
tove = 'a species of badger with smooth white hair, long hind legs, and short horns like a stag'
wabe = 'side of a hill'

Analogously, there are infinitely many potential signifieds that are not captured by the existing signifiers of a specific language such as English. Here are a few other examples of potential signifieds not captured by existing English words, as far as I know:

Signifier	Signified
?	'the hole in a coffee mug handle'
?	'body temperature below normal (above normal it is called *fever*)'
?	'a half-full container or receptacle'
?	'the piece of skin separating the nostrils'

However, even though gaps exist, humans have the ability to fill them any time they wish. They do this typically by inventing new signs, by altering already existing ones to meet new demands, by borrowing signs from other cultures, and so on. One can always find ways to refer, for instance, to the above signifieds by paraphrase or some other verbal strategy. But the lack of signifiers to encode these concepts in a direct way implies that they will not be anticipated by speakers of English within the everyday scheme of things. They are thus beyond perception.

The foregoing discussion in no way purports to lay out a theory of mind. In my view, the WH simply acknowledges something that semioticians have always taken for granted to varying degrees – namely, that the semiosphere shapes human thinking. In actual fact, creative forces are constantly at work in individual human beings. The Neapolitan philosopher Giambattista Vico (1688–1744) termed these the *fantasia* and the *ingegno*. The former is the capacity that allows human beings to imagine literally anything they desire freely and independently of biological or cultural processes; it is the creative force behind new thoughts, new ideas, new art, new science, and so on. The latter is the capacity to convert new thoughts and ideas into representational structures – metaphors, stories, works of art, scientific theories, and the like. So, although human beings are indeed shaped by the cultural system in which they are reared, they are also endowed with creative faculties that allow them to transcend it and even change that very system.

Culture can be compared to the default mode of computer software. A computer is formatted in a way that is known as its default mode. This format can, of course, be changed intentionally by a human programmer. But if no changes are made, the computer will automatically operate according to its original format. Analogously, the interconnected network of codes that constitutes a culture is the default mode for knowing the world. But in the same way that a human programmer can always choose to change a computer's format, so too, the individual human being can always decide to alter his or her own 'format' at any time. Therein lies the paradox of the human condition – throughout the life cycle, there is an unexplainable need within each individual to transcend the categories of knowing provided by existing sign systems. Changes to the format are what lead cumulatively to cultural evolution. Sign systems undergo constant change in response to any new need or demand that humans may have.

4.6 Further Reading and Online Resources

Further Reading

Andrews, Edna. *Markedness Theory*. Durham, NC: Duke University Press, 1990.
Arnheim, Rudolf. *Visual Thinking*. Berkeley: University of California Press, 1969.
Battistella, E.L. *Markedness: The Evaluative Superstructure of Language*. Albany, NY: SUNY Press, 1990.
Eco, Umberto. *Semiotics and the Philosophy of Language*. Bloomington: Indiana University Press, 1984.

– *A Theory of Semiotics*. Bloomington: Indiana University Press, 1976.
Frye, Northrop. *The Great Code: The Bible and Literature*. Toronto: Academic Press, 1981.
Lévi-Strauss, Claude. *Myth and Meaning: Cracking the Code of Culture*. Toronto: University of Toronto Press, 1978.
Whorf, Benjamin Lee. *Language, Thought, and Reality*. Ed. J.B. Carroll. Cambridge, MA: MIT Press, 1956.

Online Resources

Perhaps the best online resource for getting more information on codes, given also its various hyperlinks, is Daniel Chandler's *Semiotics for Beginners* website: http://www.aber.ac.uk/media/Documents/S4B/sem08.html.

5 Texts

Great speeches have always had great soundbites. The problem now is that the young technicians who put together speeches are paying attention only to the soundbite, not to the text as a whole, not realizing that all great soundbites happen by accident, which is to say, all great soundbites are yielded up inevitably, as part of the natural expression of the text. They are part of the tapestry, they aren't a little flower somebody sewed on.

Peggy Noonan (b. 1950)

5.1 Introduction

As something standing for something else, a sign can take any form, or 'size,' as long as it does not violate the structure of the code to which it belongs and as long as it conveys a specific type of meaning in some recognizable way. A sign can thus be something 'small,' physically speaking, such as a word or two fingers raised vertically (e.g., the V-sign, §1.1); or it can be something much 'larger,' such as an equation or a narrative. When we show the equation $c^2 = a^2 + b^2$ to a mathematician, he or she will instantly recognize it as a specific form standing for the Pythagorean theorem ('the square on the hypotenuse of a right-angled triangle is equal to the sum of the squares on the other two sides'), not as a combination of unrelated variables (letter signs). If we were to ask someone who has just read a novel what he or she got out of it, we would receive an evaluation of its overall message, not an interpretation or analysis of its separate words and parts.

In semiotic theory, 'larger signs' such as equations and novels are called *texts*; and the meanings or 'larger signifieds' that they encode are called *messages*. Texts include conversations, poems, myths, novels, television programs, paintings, scientific theories, and musical compositions. A novel, for instance, is a verbal text constructed with 'smaller' language signs (which are, more accurately, the 'signifiers' of the text) in order to communicate some overarching message (the 'larger signified'). Texts are not constructed or interpreted in terms of the meanings of their constituent parts (the smaller signs), but holistically as single forms. Codes provide the signs for constructing and interpreting texts. For example, novels are constructed and interpreted primarily on the basis of the relevant narrative code. Using Saussurean theory, it can be said that the code constitutes a form of *langue* (the abstract knowledge of how certain signs and their relations can be used and interpreted), and that the text created on the basis of the code is a form of *parole* (the concrete utilization of the code to represent something).

This chapter will look at the concept of text in semiotics. Given the vast array of texts that characterize human representational activity, the discussion here will necessarily have to be selective. The types of texts used as cases in point will be narrative (§5.3) and visual (§5.4).

5.2 What Is a Text?

A text is, as mentioned, a composite structure consisting of smaller sign elements. It is, thus, structurally isomorphic to the smaller signs that comprise it. For example, a verbal text has the same structural features as the words and sentences that constitute it – it is, in effect, a 'larger verbal sign.' But the overall meaning we get from a text is not equivalent simply to the aggregate meanings of its constituent signs. It constitutes a 'larger signified,' as it was called above.

So, how de we extract meaning (the larger signified) from texts? It would seem that we interpret texts essentially in one of two ways – *linearly* or *holistically*. Some texts can only be deciphered by means of a sign-by-sign interpretation process. This is how we read numbers in the decimal system, equations, and virtually any text written in language. Such texts are composed in a linear fashion and require a step-by-step deciphering process. Numbers, for example, are read in a linear fashion; their overall value is then determined on the basis of the values of the positions in which each of their digits occur. In this case, interpretation is cumulative; that is, the value of the entire number (= the text) is gleaned by assessing the values of the individual signs (= the digits in the number). Take, for instance, how we determine the value (= overall meaning) of the numbers 82 and 28, which are made with the same digits but in reverse order:

Value of 82:
8   ←   *value* = 80
2   ←   *value* = 2
Total value: 80 + 2

Value of 28:
2   ←   *value* = 20
8   ←   *value* = 8
Total value: 20 + 8

Analogously, to extract meaning from a narrative, we must first listen to or read the narrative, in a linear word-by-word, sentence-by-sentence fashion until the end, constructing the meaning of the text as we go along. However, as we saw in the previous chapter (§4.4), determining the larger signified in this case is not a simple linear process; it involves knowledge of oppositions inherent in the narrative code selected to construct the text. More will be said about narrative texts later on (§5.3).

Other texts are deciphered holistically, that is, by assessing their constituent parts not one at a time but rather as elements of a 'whole.' This is how we interpret a painting or appreciate a piece of music – not by looking at or listening to the component parts one-by-one but holistically. The American philosopher Susanne Langer (1895–1985) referred to the linear interpretation of texts as a *discursive* process and to the holistic interpretation of texts as a *presentational* process.[1] Discursive texts have a salient feature that can be called 'detachment,' which simply means that their constituent signs can be considered separately – for example, one can focus on a digit in a number or on a single word in a novel, detaching it from its location in the text, without impairing the overall understanding of the text. In contrast, the elements in presentational texts cannot be detached from the texts without impairing the overall meaning – for example, one cannot detach a note or phrase from a melody without destroying the sense of the melody.

The relation between the structure of a text and its interpretation has become a key area of research in semiotics. Especially interesting is the 'location' of a text's meaning, so to speak. Does it lie in the intentions of the makers of texts – the author, the composer, or the artist? And, consequently, is successful interpretation of the text on the part of the 'reader' a straightforward matter of determining the maker's intentions? Or does the meaning of the text reside instead in the reader, regardless of the maker's intentions? Umberto Eco (§1.2) has written at length on this very fascinating topic, suggesting that although infinite interpretations of the same text are possible according to reader variables, in reality the nature of the text itself and the author's intentions constrain the range of interpretations. When a given interpretation goes beyond this range, other people tend to evaluate it as erroneous, extreme, far-fetched, or implausible.

Textuality – the ability to produce and comprehend texts – is, surprisingly, found in other species, at least in terms of the above rudimentary definition of text as a composite form. Animal texts are actually complex signal formations rather than texts in the strictly human sense. One well-known example is the so-called honeybee dance. Worker honeybees returning to the hive from foraging trips inform the other bees in the hive about the direction, distance, and quality of the food with amazing accuracy through movement sequences that biologists call 'dances,' in obvious analogy to human dancing. The remarkable thing about a honeybee dance is that it appears to share with human textuality and semiosis generally the feature of displacement – that is, the feature of conveying information in the absence of the referential domain to which it calls attention. A worker bee called a 'scout' dances a figure-8 pattern up the honeycomb to show the location of the distant nectar. The more rapidly the bee dances, the nearer the food is located. The imaginary line between the loops of the 8 indicates the position of the nectar in relation to the sun:

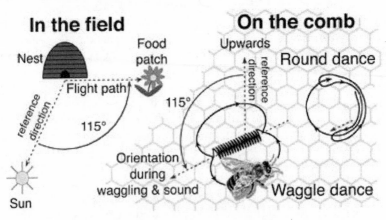

(P. Kirk Visscher, University of California, Riverside)

Several kinds of honeybee dance patterns have been documented by entomologists. In the 'round' dance, the bee moves in circles alternately to the left and to the right. This dance is apparently deployed when the cache of food is nearby. When the food source is farther away, then the bee dances in a 'wagging' fashion, moving in a straight line while wagging its abdomen from side to side and then returning to its starting point. The straight line in this dance points in the direction of the food source, the energy level indicates how rich the food source is, and the tempo provides information about its distance. In one experimental study, a feeding dish placed 330 metres from the hive triggered a dance that consisted of 15 complete rounds in 30 seconds, whereas a dish located 700 metres away triggered a dance that consisted of only 11 runs carried out in the same period of time.[2]

Despite possessing the property of detachment, such animal texts are purely referential, designating exactly what they portray – distances, orientations, and so on. Human texts, on the other hand, are both referential and connotative. There are two main ways in which connotation is built into human texts. One is called *subtextuality*, which is the embedding of a text within the main text through allusion (indirect reference); the other is called *intertextuality*, which is the text's connection to other texts mainly through inference, implication, or suggestion. For example, allusions to religious themes abound in novels, making their decipherment dependent on knowledge of the culture's religious referents. Extracting a meaning from John Bunyan's (1628–88) novel *Pilgrim's Progress* is contingent on knowing the Bible narrative, since it constitutes an allegorical tale of a Christian's journey from the City of Destruction to the Celestial City. Analogously, James Joyce's (1882–1941) novel *Ulysses* takes its title from parallels Joyce established between the adventures of his main character, Leopold Bloom, and those of Homer's Ulysses (Odysseus in Greek), who is the hero of *The Odyssey*. Bloom suffers ridicule because he is Jewish and has peculiar sexual tastes and because his wife Molly is unfaithful. He survives the pain and sorrow of his life through a remarkable capacity to absorb suffering – and even to enjoy it. The action in the novel happens over a single day – 16 June 1904, in Dublin, Ireland. The three main characters are Bloom, an advertising salesman, his wife, Molly, and young Stephen Dedalus. They are counterparts of Ulysses, his wife Penelope, and their son Telemachus, in the Greek epic. Bloom's one-day adventures in Dublin mirror the many years of wanderings Ulysses endures as he tries to return home to Ithaca after fighting in the Trojan War. *Ulysses* is one of the most challenging novels ever written because of its dense intertextuality. It is filled with intertextual references to many areas of knowledge, including theology, mythology, astronomy, Irish legends, history, and such languages as Hebrew, Latin, and Gaelic.

The notions of subtext and intertext were introduced into semiotics by Barthes and elaborated subsequently by the French semiotician Julia Kristeva (b. 1941).[3] As Barthes pointed out, a text is constituted by bits of codes, various conventional formulas, and specific kinds of discourses, all of which pass into the text and are reconfigured within it. For Barthes, then, the text is a blend of unconscious or automatic quotations, but without quotation marks.[4] For Kristeva, too, a text is more than the result of a single author's efforts – it is the result of other texts converging on it through the author's own unconscious memory. Any text is, thus, the result of an author absorbing and transforming other texts.

Work on text theory started proliferating in the early 1980s – an understandable occurrence, given the importance of texts in all areas of human representation, from mathematics and science to recreational reading. Since then, several interesting notions have emerged. A *paratext*, for example, is defined as the physical and conventional characteristics associated with certain kinds of texts. Paratextual features include such things as physical structure, titles, headings, prefaces, epigraphs, dedications, acknowledgments, footnotes, illustrations, dust jackets, and so on. An *architext* is the prototype from which similar texts are derived – for example, a classical symphony with four movements (fast–slow–medium-fast) is the architext on which most symphonies are based as replicas, modifications, elaborations, and so forth. A *metatext* is a text that makes an explicit or implicit critical commentary on another text. A *hypotext* is a text based on another text, which, however, it alters, elaborates, or extends. Parodies, spoofs, sequels, and translations are all examples of hypotexts. Finally, a *hypertext* is a text within a main text that is designed to explain it or to provide further information about some of its components.

The latter term requires further commentary, since it has become a crucial notion in this age of Internet and other forms of digital communication. Reading a printed page involves, at a basic level, deciphering the actual signs on the page. This is, as mentioned, a linear process, since it consists in decoding the individual words and their combinations in sentences. Also as mentioned, information about any specific sign in the text must be sought out in a detached fashion. For example, if one wants to follow up on a reference or meaning in the text, one has to do it physically by consulting other texts. This is of course what must be done when, for instance, one wants to look up the meaning of a word found in a text in a dictionary. Computer technology has greatly facilitated such tasks by introducing a hypertextual dimension to texts. The term *hypertext* was coined in 1965 to describe an interlinked text, which a user can access instantly by means of a simple 'clicking' procedure on the screen. This was made possible by the invention of *hyperlinks* – portions of a document that can be linked to other related documents. By clicking on the hyperlink, the user is immediately connected to the document specified by the link. Web pages are written in a simple computer language called HTML (hypertext markup language). A series of instruction 'tags' are inserted into pieces of ordinary text to control the way the page looks and can be manipulated when viewed with a Web browser. Tags determine the typeface or act as instructions to display images; they can also be used to link up with other Web pages.

As opposed to the textuality of paper-produced books, hypertextuality permits the user to browse through related topics, regardless of the presented order of the topics. For example, 'navigating' among the links to the word *language* in an article contained on a website might lead the user to the *International Phonetic Alphabet*, the science of *linguistics*, samples of languages, and so on. Hypertextuality was introduced as a regular feature of computer systems in 1987 when Apple began distributing a new program called Hypercard with its new PCs. This was the first program to provide a linking function permitting navigation among files of computer print text and graphics by clicking keywords or icons. By 1988, compact disc players were built into computers, which introduced CD-ROMs and thus hypertextuality broadly. Incidentally, in no way does hypertextuality impugn the basic linearity of printed texts. In writing a computer hypertext, the author must still lay out his or her ideas in a linear fashion and then choose which ones should be highlighted for clicking.

The notion of hypertext has some interesting implications for the psychology of text interpretation. At one level, successful interpretation entails knowing the codes with which the text has been assembled. For instance, if a verbal text is written in Finnish, in order to derive any meaning from it, the decoder must know the Finnish language, the conceptual metaphors that characterize Finnish modes of speaking, and so on and so forth. This can be called the level of the 'textual signifier.' At a different (conceptual) level, successful interpretation involves knowledge of how signification unfolds in the specific text – that is, of how the text generates its meanings through a series of internal and external signifying processes. This requires knowledge of cultural codes other than the strictly verbal or non-verbal ones used to physically create the text. This constitutes the level of the 'textual signified,' as it can be called. At this level, we ask ourselves the question: 'What does it mean?' Finally, various contextual factors enter into the entire process to constrain the interpretation, such as what the individual reader will get from it, what the intent of the author was, and so on. The interaction of these dimensions guides the extraction of meaning from the text. A little reflection will reveal that this entire process is hypertextual in nature because the reader of the text must possess the ability not only to understand its 'surface textual signifiers,' but also to navigate through the various codes that it harbours. This type of 'mental clicking,' as it can be called, is analogous to what is done on a computer screen by clicking keywords and icons physically. In effect, the structure of hypertextuality on the computer screen may well constitute a kind of 'mirror model' of how people interpret texts psychologically.

For the sake of historical accuracy, it should be mentioned that the first to become interested seriously in the theory of texts from a semiotic perspective were the so-called Russian Formalists and the Prague School linguists. Russian Formalism was rooted in two centres, the Petrograd Society for the Study of Poetic Language (*Opoyaz*), from 1916 to 1930, and the Moscow Linguistic Circle, from 1915 to 1921. The two main centres today are Moscow in Russia and Tartu in Estonia. The Prague Linguistic Circle, which was established in 1926, included members such as Nikolay Trubetzkoy and Roman Jakobson (§3.5). Taking his cue from the linguist Otto Jespersen (1860–1943), Jakobson saw signs as 'shifters' that point to the context of an utterance. The notion of shifter led him to devise a model of communication in the 1960s that continues to be widely used in contemporary semiotics and linguistics. Jakobson started by identifying six basic constituents that define communication:

1. An addresser who initiates a communication.
2. A message that the addresser wishes to convey and that he or she recognizes must refer to something other than itself.
3. An addressee who is the intended receiver of the message.

4. A context that provides the framework for encoding and decoding the text – for example, the phrase *Help me* takes on a different meaning depending on whether it is uttered by someone lying motionless on the ground or by someone in a classroom who is working on a difficult math problem.
5. A mode of contact (face to face, phone, etc.) by which the text is delivered between an addresser and an addressee.
6. A code (such as language or gesture) that provides the signs for encoding and decoding texts and their messages.

Jakobson then suggested that each of these correlates with a different communicative or expressive function:

1. *Emotive*. This is the intent of the addresser in the communication act.
2. *Conative*. This is the effect the message has (or is intended to have) on its receiver.
3. *Referential*. This is any message that is constructed to convey information (*Main Street is two blocks north of here*).
4. *Poetic*. This is any message constructed to deliver meanings iconically or poetically (*I like Mike*).
5. *Phatic*. This is any habitualized communal message designed to establish, acknowledge, or reinforce social relations (*Hi, how's it going?*).
6. *Metalingual*. This is any message that refers to the code used (*The word noun is a noun*).

Jakobson's model suggests that the creation of texts goes well beyond a simple information function. Who says what to whom, where and when it is said, and how and why it is said are all directive of the structure and utilization of textuality and communication – that is, there must always be an addresser (the maker of the text), who has a purpose for making the text (emotivity); an addressee, who is influenced by it in some way (conativity); and so on. As simple as this model appears to be, it nevertheless provides a powerful framework for discussing and understanding all kinds of texts.

Today, the branch of semiotics that aims to study texts is called, generally, *hermeneutics*. But hermeneutics is actually an ancient discipline. It began with Plato, who referred to it when discussing divination. The defining methodological feature of classical hermeneutics was an approach that saw the text as having the two levels discussed above: a surface (signifier) level consisting of constituent forms (sentences, words, phrases, etc.), and a deep (signified) level, which contains its true (sometimes called 'hidden') meanings. One of the more controversial approaches to contemporary hermeneutics is known as *deconstruction*, initiated by the late Jacques Derrida (§3.5). For Derrida, Saussure's notion of binary opposition applies to all types of textual forms, whether we realize it or not. Simply put, for Derrida each of the elements constituting a text assumes semiotic value only on the basis of its opposition to other elements. This being the case, there is no meaning outside the structure of the text. Its words can only refer to other words, and thus statements about any text subvert their own meanings. In deconstruction, there is no meaning to be found in the actual text – only the various and often mutually irreconcilable sets of oppositions constructed by readers in their search for meaning. Deconstructing these meanings (taking them apart) is the essence of Derridean hermeneutics.

As mentioned in a previous chapter (§3.5), Derrida's views took centre stage for several decades (from the early 1960s to the mid-1990s), but started losing their luster in the late 1990s, as other views of textuality came forward to challenge deconstruction theory. One of these was the concept of the semiosphere, as brought forward by the Tartu School of semiotics (§4.5). This view posits that texts gain meaning because of their interconnectedness to other texts in cultural contexts, not through some individualistic, reader-based process. As a concrete example of what this entails, consider how verbal texts (sentences) built on an *up–down* image schema (§3.3), such as *I'm feeling up, They're feeling down, I'm working my way up the ladder of success*, and *His status has gone down considerably*, are interconnected to non-verbal texts in the semiosphere. In religious symbolism, for instance, goodness, spirituality, and heaven are portrayed as *up*, and evil, damnation, and hell as *down* in sermons, theological narratives, religious visual representations, the design of churches, and the like. In public building design, too, the same schema can be discerned in the fact that the taller office buildings in a modern city are the ones that indicate which institutions (and individuals) hold social and economic power. In mathematical and scientific representational practices its occurrence can be seen, for instance, in the ways in which graphs are designed – lines that are oriented in an upward direction indicate growth or an increase of some kind, while those that are slanted in a downward direction indicate a decline or decrease. These are just some of the textual practices that are built on the *up–down* schema. The point is that such practices are all linked semiotically to one another throughout the semiosphere. They cannot be deconstructed as simple reifications of some inbuilt opposition.

5.3 Narrative Texts

Texts are created for a variety of social, intellectual, and other motives. Laws, scientific theories, movies, TV programs – and the list could go on and on – are all texts of one type or the other that serve a host of functions, from regulating social interaction to providing situations perceived as recreational. One of the most common functions of texts is storytelling as a form of self-analysis, historical consolidation, and so on. The *narrative* text is a central target in current semiotic practice. The branch devoted to its analysis is called *narratology*, a term proposed originally by the semiotician Tzvetan Todorov (b. 1939).[5] Narratology is based on the idea that narrative texts are implanted in a universal code that generates stories that vary only in detail, not in substance.

As mentioned in the previous chapter, Vladimir Propp (§4.4) was among the first semioticians to put forward this view with his analysis of Russian folktales. Propp argued, moreover, that ordinary discourse is built on the same units that make up the narrative code. In short, narrativity undergirds both conversations and fictional texts. This idea was pursued, as we saw, by Greimas (§4.4).

According to Greimas, the general flow of narrativity tends to proceed as follows (in a highly simplified way for the sake of argument):

In a typical story, there is ...
↓
a subject (the hero of the plot)
↓
who desires an object (a sought-after-
person, a magic sword, etc.)
↓
who encounters an opponent (a villain,
a false hero, a trial situation, etc.)
↓

and then finds a helper (a donor)
↓
who then gets an object from a sender
(a dispatcher)
↓
giving it to a receiver
↓
leading to a conclusion

In order to explain the passage from one narrative component to another – these components, as we saw, are called actants (§4.4) – Greimas posited a 'generative trajectory' by which the actants are projected onto the actual narration in a specific way (according to language and culture). An actant can be converted into various fundamental roles along a certain number of specified positions in its trajectory. At the actual level of telling, one actant can be represented by several characters, and several actants by one and the same character. In a mystery novel, for instance, the subject, or hero, may have several enemies, all of whom function actantially as a single opponent. In a love story, a male lover may function as both object and sender. A simple example of how actantial theory might be applied to a novel such as *Madame Bovary* by Gustave Flaubert (1821–80) goes something like this: *subject* = Emma, *object* = happiness, *sender* = romantic literature, *receiver* = Emma, *helper* = Léon, Rodolphe, *opponent* = Charles, Yonville, Rodolphe, Homais, Lheureux. The actants and the oppositions they entail are, on close analysis, the same ones found in the ancient myths. It follows that as the foundational narrative texts of humanity, myths continue to provide the subtexts and intertexts that constitute narrativity.

What is a myth? The word derives from the Greek *mythos*, 'word,' 'speech,' 'tale of the gods.' It is a fundamental form of sense making in which the characters are gods, heroes, and mystical beings; the plots are about heroes, the origins of things, or meaningful human experiences; the settings involve metaphysical worlds juxtaposed against the real world; and the narrator is an unknown being from beyond the human sphere. Myths constitute 'metaphysical knowledge texts' for explaining human origins and actions.

Interestingly, the need for myth has hardly disappeared from human societies. Myth is the form of narrative to which we instinctively resort even today for imparting knowledge of the world to children. Figures such as the Tooth Fairy and Santa Claus are just two examples of mythical characters that we continue to utilize with children. And even in contemporary adult life, mythical thinking continues to serve various functions. Climatologists, for example, refer to the warming of the ocean surface off the Western coast of South America that occurs every four to twelve years, when upwelling of cold, nutrient-rich water does not occur, as *El Niño*, 'the Christ Child' in Spanish. This creation of a *meteorological character* to represent a climatological referent makes the referent much more understandable. People do not think of *El Niño* literally as a person, nonetheless they find it convenient to blame or thank 'Him' rather than some abstract process for certain weather conditions. This mirrors, no doubt, how the original mythic characters were imagined – the difference being that the mythic characters of the past were believed to be real beings, not narrative models of physical events.

Each character in ancient myth is a sign standing for some human quality, idea, emotion, need, or intrinsic reality. Take, for example, the Greek and Roman gods. As the list below shows, each one represented something in nature or human society. Each character was, in effect, an 'embodied' or 'personified' concept or idea:

- Zeus (Jupiter) = sky god, wielder of thunderbolts; ruler of the gods. Zeus was, essentially, a sky and weather god associated with rain, thunder, and lightning.
- Poseidon (Neptune) = god of the sea and of earthquakes (brother of Zeus).
- Hades (Pluto) = god of the underworld and dispenser of earthly riches. Hades was also the god associated with death.
- Hestia (Vesta) = virgin goddess of the hearth fire.
- Demeter (Ceres) = goddess of grain and of fertility.
- Hera (Juno) = goddess of marriage and childbirth, consort of Zeus.
- Ares (Mars) = god of war.
- Apollo (Apollo) = god of archery, prophecy, music, healing, and youth.
- Artemis (Diana) = virgin goddess of archery, wild animals, and the hunt (twin sister of Apollo).
- Hermes (Mercury) = herald and messenger of the gods; god of business, god of thieves; guide of the dead to the underworld.
- Athena (Minerva) = virgin goddess of wisdom, practical arts, and war.

- Hephaestus (Vulcan) = god of fire and metalworking.
- Dionysus (Bacchus) = god of wine and fertility.
- Aphrodite (Venus) = goddess of love, sexual desire, and beauty.

An insightful discussion of myth, from the perspective of semiotic theory, is the one put forward by the anthropologist Claude Lévi-Strauss (§3.2), who saw myth as the original source for the oppositional structure of all codes. The oppositional clusters in myth are thus built into all kinds of meaning systems and institutions. Here are a few of the most common ones, according to Lévi-Strauss:

Concept	Opposite
good	evil
right	wrong
mother	father
god	devil
female	male
day	night
life	death
oneness/unity	nothingness
heaven	hell

Lévi-Strauss's view of the mythic structure of culture generally and of the systems of representation within it actually has a commonsense flavour to it. If we were to be asked what *evil* is, we would tend to explain it in terms of its opposite (*good*), and vice versa. Similarly, if we wanted to explain the concept of *right* to someone, we would invariably tend to bring up the opposite concept of *wrong* at some point. Crucial to Lévi-Strauss's conception of myth, then, is the Saussurean notion of *value* (*valeur*). Saussure argued that forms (signs), instead of carrying intrinsic meaning, have value only in differential relation to other forms. To determine the value of an American quarter, for instance, what must be known is (1) that the coin can be exchanged for a certain quantity of something different (e.g., a piece of candy) and (2) that its value can be compared with another value in the same system (e.g., with two dimes and one nickel, or with a coin belonging to another system, such as a coin in the Euro system).

The study of narrativity within semiotics today includes examining narrative structure in broader terms. Does language have a 'narrative deep structure'? Do the parts of speech originate in mythic oppositions? These are just two of the fascinating questions that this new study of narrativity asks. For some reason, however, this line of inquiry has not yet caught on in linguistics generally, which continues to view grammar (and especially syntax) as an abstract system of rule relations rather than as a product of narrative structure. Nevertheless, the conceptual metaphor movement within linguistics (§3.3) has started changing this state of affairs, as linguists become more and more aware of the effects of metaphorical (and mythical) thinking on the categories of language.

5.4 Visual Texts

The study of *visual texts* became central to semiotic theory after the publication of two influential books: Rudolf Arnheim's *Visual Thinking* (1969) and John Berger's *Ways of Seeing* (1972).[6] These brought to the attention of all semioticians the crucial role that visual representation plays in people's attempts to understand the world.

Drawing pictures, making charts, sketching diagrams, and the like are such common everyday activities that we hardly ever realize what they imply. Consider, for instance, what can be accomplished with three straight lines of equal length, one stacked above the other:

Can they be combined in some way to create recognizable figures? Indeed, they can be joined in specific configurations to represent by resemblance (iconicity) a triangle, the letter H, or a picnic table (among other things):

| triangle | the letter 'H' | picnic table |

Notice that we perceive these figures as wholes rather than as amalgams of three parts – the original three lines (see §5.2). The whole is greater than the sum of its parts, textually speaking. All visual texts are constructed and interpreted in this way – anything that can be perceived visually can be represented iconically by a combination of points, lines, and shapes. For example, a cloud can be represented as a shape and a horizon as a line. Lines, points, and shapes are the basic visual signifiers that we use to assemble visual texts. Other visual signifiers include *value, colour,* and *texture*. Value refers to the darkness or lightness of a line or shape. It plays an important role in the portrayal of contrasts, such as dark vs light. In the drawing below, dark lines are used to suggest that this particular cloud will bring about an overcast condition:

Colour conveys mood, feeling, and atmosphere in a visual text such as a painting. This is why we speak of 'warm,' 'soft,' 'cold,' and 'harsh' colours. Needless to say, each colour is a sign that has culture-specific connotations: for example, in American culture *yellow* connotes cowardice, while in China it connotes royalty.

Texture is the use of visual forms to evoke certain sensations. Wavy lines, for example, tend to produce a much more pleasant sensation in a viewer than do angular ones. When we increase the number of edges on angular lines, the unpleasant sensation tends to increase proportionately:

pleasant sensation

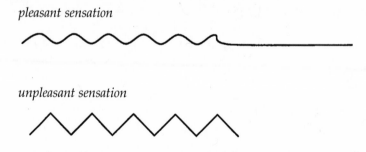

unpleasant sensation

This suggests that visual representation is intermodal, eliciting various sensory modalities in tandem. The term used to characterize this phenomenon is *synesthesia*, which is defined as the evocation of one sensation by another, as when a loud noise produces the image of a blinding light, or vice versa.

Lines and shapes can also be combined to create three-dimensional figures, which are visual texts constructed in such a way as to create an illusion of depth. The following figure is drawn with twelve lines. The way they are put together makes us perceive the figure as a three-dimensional box:

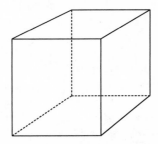

Although the figure has been drawn on a two-dimensional surface, we cannot help but perceive it as a three-dimensional box. This is because it has been drawn with the technique of 'perspective drawing,' which dupes us, in effect, into perceiving objects as having three dimensions. The flat surface is known as the *picture plane*; the horizon line is called the horizontal *eye-level line* that divides the scene in the distance; and the *vanishing point* (A) is located on the horizon line where parallel lines in the scene appear to converge. This makes certain parts of the figure appear to be closer than others:

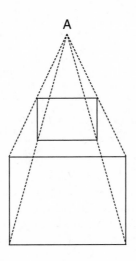

Put simply, perspective drawing is the technique for creating an illusion of depth in two-dimensional surface drawings. As a historical footnote, it dates back to the Renaissance, after the Italian artist Filippo Brunelleschi (1377–1446) used it in his own paintings, although elements of perspective drawing go right back to the ancient world. Roman artists, for instance, employed perspective, shading, and shadows to make paintings of columns and other architectural elements that continue to fool the eye with their realism to this day.

Two other types of visual texts have been targets of great interest in semiotics: *diagrams* and *charts*. A diagram is a schematic drawing that uses basic visual elements (points, lines, shapes) to 'explain' visually how something works or to clarify the relationship between the parts of some whole. A chart is a type of diagram that contains or displays information of various kinds. Diagrams are cognitively powerful visual texts. They are indispensable in science and, typically, are the sum and substance of theory making. The diagram of the atom as a miniature solar system with a nucleus and orbiting particles is, ipso facto, a theory of the atom that allows us to envision it in a particular way. Take, as an example, how three well-known atomic theories in physics can, in effect, be represented in diagram form: (1) the *Rutherford Model*, which portrays the atom space as a tiny solar system; (2) the *Bohr Model*, which adds 'quantized' orbits to the *Rutherford Model*; and (3) the *Schrödinger Model*, which posits that electrons occupy regions of space.

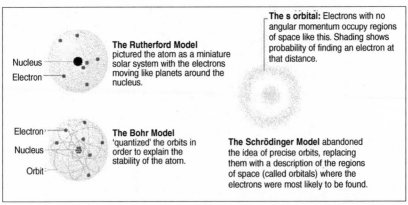

Nucleus
Electron

The Rutherford Model pictured the atom as a miniature solar system with the electrons moving like planets around the nucleus.

The s orbital: Electrons with no angular momentum occupy regions of space like this. Shading shows probability of finding an electron at that distance.

Electron
Nucleus
Orbit

The Bohr Model 'quantized' the orbits in order to explain the stability of the atom.

The Schrödinger Model abandoned the idea of precise orbits, replacing them with a description of the regions of space (called orbitals) where the electrons were most likely to be found.

The way in which each diagram is composed is hardly haphazard: each one attempts to show atomic structure according to specific types of experimental data. The referential domain is the same in all three cases – namely, atomic structure. However, each diagram provides, literally, a different 'mental view' of the same domain – a domain that is not directly accessible to vision. The *Bohr Model* is an extension of the *Rutherford* one, and the *Schrödinger Model* an extension of the earlier two. The model envisioned by Rutherford, in which electrons move around a tightly packed, positively charged nucleus, successfully explained the results of scattering experiments but was unable to explain atomic emission (i.e., why atoms emit only certain wavelengths of light). Bohr began with Rutherford's diagram but then postulated further that electrons can only move in certain quantized orbits. His model was thus able to explain certain qualities of emission for hydrogen, but failed for other elements. Schrödinger's model, in which electrons are described not by the paths they take but rather by the regions where they are most likely to be found, can explain certain qualities of emission spectra for all elements.

Charts synthesize information so that we can detect any pattern within the information. Take, for example, the following collection of numbers. They represent, in no particular order, the hypothetical number of pets in each of the households of **25** families living in a particular suburb of a city:

1, 2, 0, 4, 1, 3, 3, 1, 2, 0, 4, 5, 2, 3, 2, 3, 2, 4, 1, 2, 3, 0, 2, 3, 1

We can glean very little from looking at this layout of the numbers. A better idea of what they indicate can be gained by grouping them into a chart that lists each different value (**x**) and its frequency (**f**) of occurrence. Such a chart is called a *frequency distribution* in statistics.

Frequency distribution

x	f
0	3
1	5
2	7
3	6
4	3
5	1
	25

The chart shows us that there are three instances of **0** pets, **5** of **1** pet, and so on. Immediately, we can see a few things that are of interest. First and foremost, we can see that most of the households (**7 + 6 = 13**) have **2** or **3** pets. This is called the *central tendency* or *central location* of the data. Statistical analysis of the data can now begin in earnest.

The Pythagoreans – the followers of Pythagoras (c. 582–c. 500 BCE) – used diagrams and charts to represent numbers, so as to extract patterns from them. For example, square integers such as 1^2 (= 1), 2^2 (= 4), 3^2 (= 9), and 4^2 (= 16) can be displayed with square arrangements of little quad figures, as shown below:

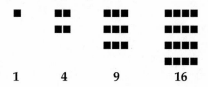

1	4	9	16

As a consequence of displaying square numbers in this way, the Pythagoreans discovered that they are equal to the sum of consecutive odd integers:

$$
\begin{aligned}
1 &= 1 \\
4 &= 1 + 3 \\
9 &= 1 + 3 + 5 \\
16 &= 1 + 3 + 5 + 7 \\
25 &= 1 + 3 + 5 + 7 + 9
\end{aligned}
$$

and so on

Why is this so? It is so because to form each new square figure, a successive odd number of quads to the preceding figure must be added – for example, to the square figure for the number **1** above, **3** new quads must be added to produce the figure for **4**; then to the square for the number **4, 5** more quads must be added to produce the next number **9**; and so on. Consider **16** as a case in point:

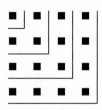

This diagram shows clearly that **16** is the sum of the first four odd numbers, since it is made up successively of **1 + 3 + 5 + 7** additions of quads. The Pythagoreans were intrigued by such findings and, consequently, studied all kinds of numbers with the same type of diagrammatic technique. Triangular numbers – numbers that can be displayed in triangular form – held a special kind of place in their numerical experiments. Here are the first four such numbers:

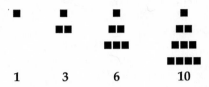

| 1 | 3 | 6 | 10 |

The number of quads in the figure for the first triangular number **1** is **1**; the number that make up the figure for the second triangular number **3** is **1 + 2**; the number of quads that make up the third triangular number **6** is **1 + 2 + 3**; and so on. Why is this so? It is so because each successive triangular number figure is obtained by adding a row of quads containing one more than the number in the bottom row of the previous triangular number:

■   ←   1   *one quad*
■■   ←   2   *one more quad than the row above*
3

■
■■   ←   2   *two quads*
■■■   ←   3   *one more quad than the row above*
6

and so on

This leads to the discovery that the nth triangular number is the sum of the first **n** counting numbers:

1st triangular number: =   1   =   1
2nd triangular number: =   3   =   1 + 2
3rd triangular number: =   6   =   1 + 2 + 3
4th triangular number: =   10   =   1 + 2 + 3 + 4

5th triangular number: =   **15**   = $1 + 2 + 3 + 4 + 5$
6th triangular number: =   **21**   = $1 + 2 + 3 + 4 + 5 + 6$
...
n^{th} triangular number: = $1 + 2 + 3 + ... + n$

These discoveries might not have been made if not for the use of visual diagrams. The formal amalgamation of arithmetic and geometric visual representation was accomplished by the French mathematician and philosopher René Descartes (1596–1650). He called his amalgamation *analytic geometry*.

5.5 Texts and Culture

In the previous chapter (§4.5), culture was defined as a system of signs – called the semiosphere – that are interconnected to one another in particular ways. In this system, texts play a primary role in how people experience culture. Without narratives, musical compositions, paintings, and the like, there would be no culture anywhere. Culture is, in a word, a 'macro-textual' system.

Texts are testaments of who we are. Some are perceived to have high value, and for this reason they are preserved for posterity – important books are preserved in libraries; paintings in galleries, musical texts in conservatories, and so on. This is so because human beings depend on texts to understand themselves and to probe questions of meaning or purpose to life. The anthropologist Clifford Geertz has perhaps best expressed the paradox of the human condition by stating wryly that without culture, human beings would be 'unworkable monstrosities, with few useful instincts, few recognizable sentiments, and no intellect.'[7] From the moment of birth, the textuality (stories, musical forms, etc.) into which individuals are born shapes their behaviour and world view. By the time children can talk, they have become creatures of their culture – its habits are their habits, its beliefs their beliefs, its challenges their challenges.

In the human species, nature and culture are intrinsically intertwined. The Polish-born British anthropologist Bronislaw Malinowski (1884–1942) argued that cultures came about so that the human species could solve similar basic physical and moral problems the world over. Malinowski saw the languages, rituals, and institutions that humans have created – no matter how strange they might at first seem – as possessing universal properties that have allowed people everywhere to solve similar life problems. The British anthropologist Alfred Radcliffe-Brown (1881–1955) noted that even a physical response like weeping can hardly be explained in purely biological terms. He found that among the Andaman Islanders in the Bay of Bengal, crying was not primarily an expression of joy or sorrow, but rather a response to social situations characterizing meaningful events such as peace making, marriage, and the reunion of long-separated intimates. In crying together, the people renewed their ties of cultural solidarity.

Finding hard scientific evidence to explain why culture emerged in the course of human evolution has proved to be a monumental challenge. Understandably, many have resorted to speculating or reasoning inferentially. What would happen if human beings were somehow forced to survive without culture? The best examples of this form of inferential thinking have, actually, come not from scientists or philosophers, but from writers of fiction. Daniel Defoe's (1660–1731) novel *Robinson Crusoe* and William Golding's (1911–93) *Lord of the Flies*, for instance, deal with intriguing fictional 'test cases' of people forced to live outside a cultural ambiance, and then infer what would happen to them and how they would respond. In all such 'cases,' a tribal-like form of living is the one that is assumed to emerge. Leaving aside the meaning of *tribe* in anthropological terms, suffice it to say here that people do seem to relate more meaningfully to smaller communities even in contemporary city-societies, in which various cultures, subcultures, counterclutures, and parallel cultures exist in constant competition with one another, and in which the shared territory is so large that it constitutes a mere abstraction. The tendency for individuals to relate to tribal groupings manifests itself regularly, on everything from cliques and gangs to workplace groupings. This inclination towards tribalism, as the great Canadian communications theorist Marshall McLuhan (1911–80) emphasized, reverberates constantly among modern-day humans living, as they do, in large, impersonal social systems.

At the core of culture lie the texts created to document its origins (myths), to indicate its direction (history), to entertain its members (fiction, dance), to ritualize events (drama, music), and so on. In the semiosphere, texts are more powerful in shaping human destiny than are genes. Each culture is, as mentioned, a macrotextual system. This is why we equate, say, Italian culture with such texts as Dante's *Divine Comedy*, Giuseppe Verdi's *Rigoletto*, and Michelangelo's *David*, among many others. Were these texts to disappear and fade from human memory at some time in the future, so would Italian culture as we know it today.

5.6 Further Reading and Online Resources

Further Reading

Allert, B., ed. *Languages of Visuality: Crossings between Science, Art, Politics, and Literature*. Detroit: Wayne State University Press, 1996.
Bal, Mieke. *Narratology: Introduction to the Theory of the Narrative*. Toronto: University of Toronto Press, 1985.
Barthes, Roland. *Image–Music–Text*. London: Fontana, 1977.
Eco, Umberto. *Interpretation and Overinterpretation*. Cambridge: Cambridge University Press, 1992.
– *The Role of the Reader: Explorations in the Semiotics of Texts*. Bloomington: Indiana University Press, 1979.
Genette, G. *Narrative Discourse Revisited*. Ithaca, NY: Cornell University Press, 1988.
Leitch, T.M. *What Stories Are: Narrative Theory and Interpretation*. University Park: Penn State University Press, 1986.
Nash, C. *Narrative in Culture*. London: Routledge, 1994.
Prince, G. *Narratology: The Form and Functioning of Narrative*. Berlin: Mouton, 1982.
Propp, Vladimir J. *Morphology of the Folktale*. Austin: University of Texas Press, 1928.
Ricoeur, Paul. *Time and Narrative*. Chicago: University of Chicago Press, 1983.
Saint-Martin, F. *Semiotics of Visual Language*. Bloomington: Indiana University Press, 1990.
Sebeok, Thomas A., and Jean Umiker-Sebeok, eds. *Advances in Visual Semiotics*. Berlin: Mouton de Gruyter, 1994.
Tufte, E.R. *Visual Explanations: Images and Quantities, Evidence and Narrative*. Cheshire: Graphics Press, 1997.

Online Resources

The *Text Semiotics* site (http://www.text-semiotics.org/english1.html) is very useful for getting information on the subject matter of this chapter, because it contains useful links to sites of interest.

6 Representation

In the final analysis, 'style' is art. And art is nothing more or less than various modes of stylized, dehumanized representation.

Susan Sontag (1933–2005)

6.1 Introduction

Before the advent of alphabets, people passed on knowledge primarily through the spoken word. But even in early oral cultures, human beings made tools for recording and preserving ideas in physically durable ways. One of these was pictography, or the representation of ideas by means of pictures. Pictography continues to be a basic (and instinctive) representational modality to this day, even though most written communication is alphabetic. The figures designating 'male' and 'female' on washrooms and the 'no smoking' signs found in public buildings, to mention but two common examples, are modern-day pictographs.

More precisely, pictography constitutes a *medium* of representation – that is, a physical means or process by which signs are encoded and transmitted. The relation between media and representation is, needless to say, of central interest to semiotics, especially as it relates to how we encode referents. Pictography did not alter the basic oral nature of everyday communication, nor did it alter early societies' oral mode of transmitting knowledge. That occurred after the invention of alphabetic writing around 1000 BCE – an event that brought about the first true transformation of human history, constituting what the American philosopher Thomas Kuhn (1922–96) called a 'paradigm shift.'[1] Alphabetic writing made the written word a universal medium for representing, storing, and exchanging ideas and knowledge. After the development of movable type technology – an event that made it possible to print and duplicate books cheaply – knowledge stored in the print medium became a universal commodity. Marshall McLuhan (§5.5) designated the global social order that ensued from that technological paradigm shift the 'Gutenberg Galaxy,' after Johannes Gutenberg (c. 1400–68) the German printer who developed movable type in Europe.[2] In the twentieth century, electronic technology came forward to provide yet another medium for communicating information, for representing ideas, and, above all else, for providing distraction to larger and larger masses of people. Since electronic signals can cross borders virtually unimpeded, McLuhan characterized the social order that crystallized as a consequence, a 'global village.' The globalization process was further entrenched towards the latter part of the twentieth century when the Internet emerged as a quick and cheap medium of communication. The 'Digital Galaxy' in which we now live has drastically altered not only how we represent knowledge but also how we perceive it.

The impact of new media on representational practices is undeniable – never before have they become such important components of everyday life, from online advertising techniques to compression writing in text messaging (§3.4). This chapter will look at the notion of representation. The basic view of most semioticians is that our representational practices serve a basic human need – to explore and understand the world in meaningful ways, no matter which medium is used to do so. Paradoxically, by representing the world, we end up changing it, making it virtually impossible for us to distinguish between reality and our representations of it.

6.2 What Is Representation?

Plays, musical compositions, poems, and other texts were defined in the previous chapter as 'larger signs' standing for 'larger signifieds.' More specifically, they can be called texts that *represent* something according to specific traditions and practices. Representation can be defined simply as the activity of making texts. It is a unique ability that has allowed us to gain autonomy from purely sensory-instinctual ways of knowing the world. When an infant comes into contact with an object, his or her first impulse is to explore it with the senses – that is, to handle it, taste it, smell it, listen to any sounds it makes, and visually observe its features. During childhood, humans (like all animals) use their sensory apparatus regularly to know or 'cognize' objects in their environment in terms of how they feel, taste, smell, and so on. The resulting sensory units stored in memory allow children to 'recognize' objects later on without having to examine them all over again with their senses. Now, as infants grow, they start to engage more and more in cognizing behaviour that clearly transcends this cognizing phase; for example, they start to point to objects, imitate any sounds they might make, and so on. This behaviour is independent of cultural conditioning; it comes with having a human brain. At that point in human development, objects start to assume a new cognitive form of existence, becoming rudimentary signs that children start exploring with their minds rather than their bodies. It is then that children start referring to the world through conversation, through sketches on paper, and through other forms of representation.

Representation is not, however, an open-ended process. It is constrained by social conventions, by communal experiences, and by other contextual factors. As an example, consider the notion of 'sex.' Sex is something that people throughout the world experience in largely similar ways, physically and emotionally speaking. Differences emerge in people's culture-specific representations of sex – representations of sex in, say, London are vastly different from representations of the same referent that tend to be made in Calcutta or San Francisco. Moreover, the medium used to portray the referent also shapes the meaning. Photographs can show fairly limited views of sexual activity, whereas movies can provide much more graphic detail. Finally, the ways in which people living in London, Calcutta, or San Francisco derive meaning from any representation vary widely. This is because they have become accustomed in their specific cultures to different views of sex. In a fundamental semiotic sense, representation is the 'in some way' part of the definition of the sign as 'something standing for something else *in some way*.'

6.3 Representation and Myth

Many types of representational practices originate in myth. Consider Superman, who was introduced in 1938 by Action Comics and published separately a little later in Superman Comic Books, discussed briefly in §4.4. What or who does Superman represent? And why is he so popular? As a hero in the tradition of ancient mythic heroes, Superman is a figment of the childhood imagination. This is why heroic figures are found in the childhood narrative traditions of cultures across the world with virtually the same kinds of characteristics. But heroes also play a role in adult traditions, representing virtues that people across the world admire as being rare, attainable only by a 'chosen few.' As a heroic figure, Superman has of course been updated and adapted culturally – he is an 'American' hero who stands for 'truth, justice, and the American way,' as the 1950s TV series used to put it. But like the ancient heroes, Superman is indestructible, morally upright, and devoted to saving humanity from itself. And like many of the mythic heroes, he has a 'tragic flaw' – exposure to 'kryptonite,' a substance found on the planet where he was born, renders him devoid of his awesome powers.

Clearly, answering the question of why Superman (or any comic book action hero, for that matter) appeals to modern-day audiences requires us to delve into the origins and history of the archetypal hero code. In mythology and legend, a hero is an individual, often of divine ancestry, who is endowed with great courage and strength, celebrated for bold exploits, and sent by the gods to Earth to play a crucial role in human affairs. Heroes are, thus, personified signs representing lofty human ideals for all to admire – truth, honesty, justice, fairness, moral strength, and so on. Modern-day audiences feel this intuitively, as did the ancient ones who watched, for example, stage performances of Aeschylus' (c. 525–456 BCE) *Prometheus Bound, Prometheus Unbound,* and *Prometheus the Fire-Bringer* in Greece. Instead of being sent by the gods from the afterworld to help humanity, Superman came to Earth from a planet in another galaxy; he leads a 'double life,' as hero and as Clark Kent, a 'mild-mannered' reporter for a daily newspaper; he is adored by Lois Lane, a reporter for the same newspaper, who suspects (from time to time) that Clark Kent may be Superman; and he wears a distinctive costume. This original pop culture 'Superman code' was (and in various versions continues to be) an adaptation of the ancient hero code.

Although the foregoing discussion is an extreme simplification of the hero code, since more than one hero code existed in mythological traditions, the main point is still a valid one – pop culture hero codes have adapted the ancient codes to suit current audiences. The gist of the semiotic story of Superman, therefore, is that he represents a 'recycled' hero – a blend of Prometheus, Hercules, Samson, and a few others of comparable heroic ilk:

The mythic hero ...	Superman ...
is sent or banished by the gods to Earth, or else comes to Earth to help humans of his own accord: for example, Prometheus stole fire from the gods and gave it to human beings. Zeus punished him by ordering him bound to a remote peak in the Caucasus Mountains.	comes from another planet.
helps humans run their affairs: for example, Prometheus stole fire from the gods and gave it to human beings.	helps 'good' people in trouble and defeats the 'bad guys.'
has a tragic flaw: for example, by cutting his hair, one could take away Samson's strength; by injuring his heel, one could overcome the strength of Achilles; and so on.	is rendered powerless and vulnerable by exposure to kryptonite, a substance found on his home planet.
exemplifies virtue, honesty, and all the ideals that humanity looks up to but that common people rarely embody.	represents 'truth,' 'justice,' 'the American way,' and all the virtues that modern-day people aspire to have but often fail to manifest.

As this example shows, pop culture representations are, more often than not, based on recycled codes dressed up in contemporary garb to appeal to contemporary audiences. All kinds of contemporary media characters, such as movie cowboys and detectives, have enduring appeal because they are modern-day versions of ancient heroic characters. Like their ancestors, modern-day people need heroes subconsciously to 'make things right' in human affairs, at least in the realm of the imagination.

As discussed throughout this book, semiotic structures and forms involve opposition. This is true of representation as well. We recognize the qualities that Superman possesses as being what they are because they contrast blatantly with those possessed by the 'villains' or 'opponents' he encounters during his many escapades:

Superman ...	His Opponent ...
is actively friendly and conscientious.	is actively hostile and unscrupulous.
is benign.	is malicious.
is selfless and considerate.	is self-serving.
embodies Goodness.	embodies Evil.
is honest, frank, and open.	is cunning, insincere, and deceitful.
is brave.	is a coward.

The colours of the costume that Superman wears are also suggestive of a type of symbolism that reaches back into the history of heroes. His red cape suggests 'noble blood' and his blue tights the 'hope' he brings to humanity. Of course, the red and blue combination is also indicative of 'American patriotism' – being the colours of the American flag. Superman embodies all the heroic virtues that human beings aspire to possess but, being weak, fail to possess.

How Superman acts, how he behaves, how he looks, and what he does are all predictable aspects of the code, no matter who tells it or in which medium it is told. The code, therefore, can be seen as providing a set of basic actants or 'sign roles' (as they may be called) and implicit instructions for making representations of Superman in comic book, television, or movie form. Some of these include the following, as we have seen above:

- Superman lives a double life as hero and as reporter Clark Kent.
- He is adored by Lois Lane. As Superman, he ignores her advances, but as Clark Kent, he shows an amorous interest in her.
- As Clark Kent, he dresses like a typical American male reporter of the era (suit and tie, hat, etc.). He changes into his Superman costume (away from the public eye) only when the situation calls for heroic intervention.
- Superman never shows favouritism. He is always straightforward and honest.
- Superman has heroic strength. He is indestructible by human means. Given his tragic flaw, he may become momentarily over-powered by some villain who comes into possession of kryptonite; even so, through serendipitous circumstances he is always able to survive and defeat the villain.
- Superman has, in sum, all the qualities and virtues of heroes.

In contemporary mass culture, many representations have a mythic origin. This includes ritualized spectacles. Take sport spectacles as an example. In these, there is the good player or team (the home team) vs the evil one (the visiting team). The entire fanfare associated with preparing for the 'big event,' such as the Superbowl of American football, has a quality to it similar to the pomp and circumstance that ancient armies engaged in before going out to battle. Indeed, the whole event is represented by the media to be a battle of mythic proportions. The symbolism of the team's (army's) uniform, the valour and strength of the players (the heroic warriors), and the skill and tactics of the coach (the army general) all have powerful effects on the fans (the warring nations).

To distinguish between the original myths and rituals and their modern-day versions, Barthes designated the latter *mythologies*.[3] In his 1957 book bearing the same title, he composed a series of twenty-eight short essays analysing common features of popular French culture (wrestling matches, ads for soap powders, toys, striptease performances, etc.), showing that they are all forms of myth.[4] A *mythology*, thus, is a type of discourse that belongs to a 'second order semiological system,' as he called it.

Popular movies, best-selling novels, sports spectacles, and the like serve similar mythological functions, being based on specific codes (such as the Superman hero code). Representations and spectacles are thus guided by unconscious or latent code features (setting, character, etc.) that define their style and form. For example, the main features of the western, sci-fi, detective, and sitcom genres can be charted as shown on the next page.

Let's consider the Hollywood western more closely. In its original prototype form, the basic plot of the western revolved around a lonesome cowboy hero who wins a 'high noon' gun duel and then rides off into the sunset. The cowboy hero has all the traits of the classic mythic heroes – strength, physical handsomeness, honesty, and vulnerability (tragic flaw). The cowboy villain has all the opposite traits – cowardice, physical ugliness, dishonesty, and cunning. The hero is beaten up at some critical stage, but against all odds he prevails through a test of superhuman strength and valour, becoming a champion of ethics and justice. Cowboy heroes such as Roy Rogers, Wyatt Earp, Hopalong Cassidy, and the Lone Ranger have become cultural icons because of what they represent – virtue, heroism, and righteousness. Although Hollywood has also showcased female characters, most of the women portrayed in westerns have traditionally

Features of the code	Western	Sci-fi	Detective	Family sitcom
Time frame	Early America	Future	Present	Present
Setting	Frontier (outside of civilization)	Space	City (usually the inner city)	Suburbs/inner city
Heroic figure(s)	Cowboy	Astronaut	Detective	Father/mother
Supporting character	Sidekick, female lover	Astronaut with romantic relation to the protagonist	Sidekick (often providing humour or contrast)	Other parent
Opponent figure(s)	Outlaw(s)	Aliens, space itself	Killer	Boss/neighbour
Secondary characters	Native Americans, townsfolk	Technicians in spacecraft	Policemen, witnesses, etc.	Children
Plot	Restore law and order	Conquer or repel aliens	Find the killer	Solve a problem
Theme	Justice and freedom	Humanity must triumph	Provide assurance that human intellect wins out over brutality	Family values
Weaponry	Guns, rifles, fists	Space guns	Gun, intellect	Insults

played a subsidiary supporting role to the virile cowboy hero. Hollywood has broken away somewhat from this pattern in recent times, with films such as Clint Eastwood's *Unforgiven* (1992); but the tradition of the maverick cowboy loner fighting for justice remains the central mythic image even in contemporary cowboy narratives.

A mythology can also lead to the establishment of lifestyle and social trends. Childhood, for instance, emerged as a mythology during the Industrial Revolution of the nineteenth century, when for the first time in history children were considered to be human beings at a stage of life as yet uncorrupted and untainted by civilization. The concept of a period of life characterized by innocence, purity, and simplicity did not exist in previous eras, nor is it a universal one today. Children are younger human beings undergoing growth in body, mind, and personality. They are different from adults, not any better or worse. The images of children as pure and innocent is part of a mythology, not a psychology or sociology of childhood. A child has no awareness whatsoever of being pure or innocent – adults do. In medieval and Renaissance paintings and portraits there are no children as such. The 'babes' that do appear occasionally in portraits look more like adult midgets than they do children. Before the Industrial Revolution, most people lived in agricultural communities or settings. Children barely out of infancy were expected to share the workload associated with tending to the farm. There was, consequently, little distinction between childhood and adult roles – children were perceived to be adults with smaller and weaker bodies. During the Industrial Revolution, the center of economic activity shifted from the farm to the city, with many moving into the city (urbanization). This led to the construction of a new social order with different social role categories. As a result, children were left with few of their previous responsibilities, and a new mythology emerged that proclaimed children to be vastly different from adults, and therefore in need of time to play, to learn at school, and so on. Child labour laws were passed and public education became compulsory. Protected from the harsh reality of industrial work, children came to assume a new, pristine identity as innocent, faultless, impressionable, malleable creatures.

Once the mythology of childhood entered cultural groupthink, it started to shape attitudes and lifestyle patterns profoundly. As a case in point of how powerful the mythology of childhood has become, let's turn the cultural clock back to the 1983 Christmas shopping season to revisit the 'Cabbage Patch doll craze' from a semiotic perspective. Hordes of parents were prepared to pay almost anything to get one of the dolls for their daughters. Scalpers offered the suddenly and unexplainably out-of-stock dolls (a marketing ploy?) for hundreds of dollars through the classified ads. Grown adults fought one another in line-ups to get one of the few remaining dolls left in stock at some mall toy outlet.

How could a simple doll have caused such mass hysteria? To a semiotician, only something imbued with mythological signification could have. It is instructive to note, incidentally, that the Cabbage Patch dolls came with 'adoption papers.' This is a concrete clue (signifier) as to what the dolls really meant semiotically. Each doll was given a name – taken at random from 1938 State of Georgia birth records – which, like any act of naming, conferred on it a personality and human existence. And thanks to computerized factories, no two dolls were manufactured alike. The doll was a 'person substitute,' an iconic sign of childhood that was adopted into the family as if it were a sibling. No wonder, then, that the Cabbage Patch episode was fraught with so much hysteria. Parents were not buying a simple doll; they were buying their child another member of the family. Toys, as the name of a major toy chain overtly puts it, are indeed us.

As a final example of how recycled mythic representations continue to have emotional power over us, consider the case of the Star Wars set of six movies, which started in 1977 and ended in 2005 under the directorship of American motion-picture director and producer George Lucas (b. 1944). Echoes of Greek dramatic style as well as Greek mythical referents abound in the set. In a Greek tragedy, the story began typically with a prologue or monologue that explains the topic of the tragedy. Each episode of Star Wars begins in the same manner through the use of rising text against the background of space: 'A long time ago in a galaxy far away ...' The Star Wars saga is also divided into individual episodes, released in a sequence that starts in medias res, with the fourth episode being the first one put out. Homer's Iliad is presented in exactly this manner.

Significantly, the unifying theme of all the episodes is the universal struggle between Evil (the tyrannical Empire) and Good (the Rebel Alliance). The villains appear in futuristic white armour that covers them from head to toe. Their leader, Darth Vader, is entirely covered in black and speaks in a low tone of voice. The common meaning associated with the White vs Dark dichotomy in Western culture is not entirely apparent in this scene; the oppositional value of this

dichotomy is present nonetheless. White and Dark are no longer portrayed as opposing sides, but rather as two sides of the same signifying coin. Darth Vader is the only figure wearing the black armour and
cape, symbolizing the fact that he is isolated as the leading figure of the
dark side.

Hero status in the set of movies cannot be attributed to one figure,
but rather to a group who must work together for good to prevail.
Luke Skywalker is one of them. As the story unfolds, Luke discovers
that his father was a Jedi Knight, protecting the Old Republic. A Jedi
Knight is a mighty warrior who can use 'the force' to prevail. Luke's
father possessed the force, and, thus, by descendancy, so does Luke.
He is the last Jedi Knight who must fight against the dark side. But he
has a tragic desire – he yearns for a father. In line with the Greek tradition of tragic irony, it is Darth Vader who turns out to be Luke's
father.

The *Star Wars* saga reverberates with ancient mythic oppositions
and themes. They are given a modern twist, but they remain essentially the same:

youth	vs	*old*	(immaturity/idealism vs maturity/wisdom)
Luke	vs	*the emperor*	(the common person vs an authority figure)
nature	vs	*technology*	(Nature vs Culture and history)
the Force	vs	*evil*	(Good vs Evil)
Jedi	vs	*Sith*	(democratic society vs totalitarianism)
rebels	vs	*empire*	(common folk vs authority)
freedom	vs	*tyranny*	(democracy vs autocracy)
love	vs	*hate*	(constructive behaviour vs destructive)
son	vs	*father*	(passage rite based on separation)

The 'twist' given to the resolution of these oppositions is, of course,
an American one. Only in America do the young triumph over the old
and do young people teach adults about love and goodness. The idea
that young people are 'purer' and less 'hypocritical' than adults and
somehow nobler than adults is a culturally based one that surfaces in
all kinds of narratives, from J.M. Barrie's (1860–1937) *Peter Pan* to J.D.
Salinger's (b. 1919) *Catcher in the Rye*.

As a morality tale, *Star Wars* has simply 'rebranded' itself as a battle
between the Jedi and the Sith. The members of the Jedi Order have

dedicated themselves for thousands of generations to mastering the knowledge and tranquility found in the benevolent light side of the Force. They have pledged their lives to the battle against evil. They have trained themselves physically and mentally to live an austere life, and they use their skills to serve the Galactic Republic as guardians of justice and protectors of peace. They settle interplanetary disputes and defend the galaxy against aggression, thus earning universal respect. They apply the Force to manipulate the minds of the weak-willed, move objects telekinetically, peer into the future, and move around at enormous speeds; and they survive death with their consciousness intact. Recalling the Biblical story of Lucifer's fall, a renegade Jedi who succumbed to the Dark side has recruited other disenfranchised Jedi to his cause and declared war on the Order. After a devastating battle, the fallen Jedi are banished, and settle on a distant planet (Korriban), where they become known as the Sith. Fuelled by hatred and by a never-ending thirst for power, the Sith clash constantly with the Jedi. The collateral damage from these battles has devastated entire star systems. The Sith believe in conquering others, drawing their strength from the Dark side of the Force, but are ultimately enslaved by the Dark Side. After a savage battle thousands of years ago, all Sith were thought to have perished. But one survived, who restructured the cult so that at most there could be only one master and one apprentice.

As the popularity of the *Star Wars* saga makes clear, myths continue to play an important role in the representational practices of contemporary societies. Indeed, we can understand much of what is happening in today's society by analysing the mythic structure of its spectacles and rituals, and especially its fictional heroes.

6.4 Representation and Reality

A philosophical question arises from all this: Is representation an attempt to encode reality, or is it necessarily an illusory practice (as Barthes would have it) designed to impart sense to life, which otherwise would have none? As discussed in chapter 3 (§3.5), deconstructionists hold the latter view of representation. The traditional structuralist would counter by saying that representational practices allow us to probe and explore reality and thus 'discover' the elements of reality – albeit often by accident or serendipity. There have in fact been countless episodes in the history of human representation during which the structuralist perspective seems to have held water.

As a case in point, consider Leonardo Fibonacci's (c. 1175–c. 1240) famous Rabbit Puzzle, which the practical-minded medieval mathematician created simply to illustrate the advantages of the decimal numeration system. As it turns out, no other puzzle has had as many implications for the study of numerical patterns; and no other puzzle has had as many 'reifications' – that is, manifestations in natural phenomena and human products. There is no evidence that Fibonacci himself understood the implications and applications that the solution to his puzzle would turn out to have. It was the French mathematician François Edouard Anatole Lucas (1842–91) who noticed some of these implications. Since Lucas's observations, the plethora of mathematical properties that the Fibonacci Sequence has been found to conceal and the number of reifications that it has been found to have in nature and in human life have been absolutely astounding. Fibonacci's puzzle leads us to ask an obvious question: How can such a simple representamen, designed originally to represent the efficiency of decimal numerals over Roman ones, contain so many 'secrets of the universe?'

As Umberto Eco has cogently argued with regard to discovery in general, the crystallization of the Fibonacci Sequence (as the solution to the Rabbit Puzzle is called) is one of those 'episodes' in human history that shows how serendipity and discovery are intertwined.[5] This episode has enormous implications for the study of representation, since it suggests that representation is hardly an arbitrary process, but one that seems to constitute an unconscious probe of reality leading, in and of itself, to the discovery of 'hidden principles' that govern human life and the universe.

Signs give shape to formless ideas, not in an arbitrary fashion, but rather in response to inferential processes that are tied to our experience of reality. Knowledge systems vary throughout the world, but on closer scrutiny, this variation is superficial. Beneath the surface of these systems are sign creation processes that reflect universals regarding how reality is perceived. The problem is that we never get the 'whole picture' at once. This is why special theories of the physical universe are possible and highly useful whereas general ones are not. In other words, our knowledge systems can only give us partial glimpses of reality. What is important to note is that the elements that constitute these systems are hardly the product of firm reasoning processes; rather, they seem to come to consciousness as if by magic. Discoveries cannot be forced by logical analysis; they simply *happen*. But such analysis is not entirely magical or random, as the Fibonacci episode shows; it is probably tied to unconscious modes of interconnecting experiences and their meanings. This is arguably the reason why a representation in one realm of knowledge leads to discoveries in other realms.

The word *serendipity*, incidentally, was coined by Horace Walpole in 1754, from the title of the Persian fairy tale 'The Three Princes of Serendip,' whose heroes make many fortunate discoveries accidentally.[6] The tale goes somewhat as follows. Three princes from Ceylon (Sri Lanka) were journeying in a strange land when they came upon a man looking for his lost camel. The princes had never seen this particular camel, but they asked the owner a series of seemingly pertinent questions: Was it missing a tooth? Was it blind in one eye? Was it lame? Was it laden with butter on one side and honey on the other? Was it being ridden by a pregnant woman? Incredibly, the answer to every one of their questions was yes. The owner instantly accused the princes of having stolen the animal since, clearly, they could not have had such precise knowledge otherwise. But the princes merely pointed out that they had observed the road, noticing that the grass on either side was uneven and that this was most likely the result of the camel eating the grass. They had also noticed parts of the grass that were chewed unevenly, suggesting a gap in the animal's mouth. The uneven patterns of footprints indicated signs of awkward mounting and dismounting, which could be related to uneven weights on the camel. Given the society of the era, this suggested the possibility that the camel was ridden by a pregnant woman, creating a lack of equilibrium and thus an uneven pattern of footprints. Finally, in noticing differing accumulations of ants and flies, they concluded that the camel was laden with butter and honey – the natural attractors of these insects. Their questions were, as it turns out, inferences based on astute observations, or to use Peircean terminology, 'abductions' of a logico-inferential nature.

Ceylon's ancient name was Serendip, and it was Walpole who, after having read the tale, decided to introduce the word *serendipity* into the English language. The princes made their discovery of the truth as a result of what Walpole called 'accidental sagacity.' Serendipity characterizes the history of discovery in mathematics and the sciences – Wilhelm Conrad Roentgen (1845–1923) accidentally discovered X-rays by seeing their effects on photographic plates; Alexander Fleming (1881–1955) serendipitously discovered penicillin by noticing the effects of a mold on bacterial cultures; and the list could go on and on. The historical record suggests that discovery is hardly the product of a systematic search for truth, but rather a serendipitous consequence of using our abductive brain.

What is perhaps even more astounding is that serendipity plays a role in reification – that is, the manifestation of a form in referential domains other than the original one in which it was forged. A perfect example of this involves the reifications of π (pi) = 3.14. π is the ratio that results when the circumference of a circle is divided by its diameter. Serendipitously, π appears in a number of mathematical calculations and formulas, such as the one used to describe the motion of a pendulum or the vibration of a string. It also turns up in equations describing rainbows, waves, navigation problems, the DNA double helix, ripples spreading from where a raindrop falls into water, and on and on. Does this mean that the circle form is implicit in these domains? What is the connecting link between the circle form that produced the notion of π and other forms such as rainbows?

In a fascinating 1998 movie, π: *Faith in Chaos*, created by the American Darren Aronofsky, a brilliant mathematician named Maximilian Cohen teeters on the brink of insanity as he searches for an elusive numerical code hidden in π. For ten years, Cohen has been on the verge of decoding the numerical pattern underlying the ultimate system of human-made chaos – the stock market. As he approaches a solution, real chaos is swallowing the world in which he lives. Pursued by an aggressive Wall Street firm set on financial domination and by a Kabbalah sect intent on unlocking the secrets hidden in their ancient holy texts, Cohen races to crack the code, hoping to defy the madness that looms before him. Instead, he uncovers a secret for which everyone is willing to kill him. As the movie's subtext implies, the stream of digits of π challenges us to find a pattern within them. What do they *represent*? The greatest challenge to date, however, has been simply to compute π further than before. The further it has been computed, the more old theories about patterns within π are dispelled and the more new ones are created. So far, π has been computed to more than 51 billion digits. What is the attraction to this number? Is it perhaps the fact that a circle is probably the most perfect and simple form known to human beings? And why does π appear in statistical forms, in biology, and in many other domains of knowledge? It simply keeps cropping up, reminding us that it is there and defying us to understand why. Very much like the universe itself, the more technologically advanced we become and the larger our picture of π grows, the more its mysteries grow. There is a beauty to π that sustains our interest in it.

The idea that signs are both reactions to experience and subsequent locators of new experiences is an extremely problematic one for many philosophers and mathematicians. Even so, it offers crucial insights for any attempt to approach (if not answer) one of the oldest questions in philosophy and mathematics: Is mathematics invented, or is it discovered? Semiotics makes it clear that, paradoxically, the answer to both questions is *yes*. As modern physics attempts to develop a 'theory of everything' from increasingly abstract mathematics, as financial markets succumb to the mystery of mathematical measures of risk, and as biology employs combinatorial algorithms to unlock the genetic code, it does not seem far-fetched to imagine that numbers do indeed hold the key to the universe. Does the cosmos make mathematics, or does mathematics make the cosmos? The differences in notation in numeration (Roman, decimal, etc.) are, of course, cultured based and invented, but the similarity of meaning of all such systems goes beyond culture. Numbers are thus both invented and discovered. The human mind creates numbers in the same way that it creates colour concepts. Yet the colours we perceive correspond to something real outside the mind. In this sense, we are discovering numbers all the time.

When all is said and done, the question of where invention ends and discovery begins and vice versa seems to defy a satisfactory answer. The case of the Fibonacci sequence is a truly remarkable one in this regard: it is at one level a simple representation of a numerical puzzle, yet it contains within its solution so many discoveries that it truly boggles the mind to arrive at a rational explanation as to why this is so.

The puzzle is found in Fibonacci's *Liber Abaci* (1202). Fibonacci designed his book as a practical introduction to the Hindu–Arabic number system, which he learned to use during his extensive travels in the Middle East. His method of exposition was involved creating puzzles to illustrate how easily the Hindu–Arabic system could be used to solve what would otherwise, with the Roman numeral system, constitute intractable problems. The puzzle is found in Section III of the *Liber Abaci:* 'A certain man put a pair of rabbits, male and female, in a very large cage. How many pairs of rabbits can be produced in that cage in a year if every month each pair produces a new pair which, from the second month of its existence on, also is productive?'

There is 1 pair of rabbits in the cage at the start. At the end of the first month, there is still only 1 pair, for the puzzle states that a pair is productive only 'from the second month of its existence on.' It is during the second month that the original pair produces its first offspring pair. Thus, at the end of the second month, a total of 2 pairs, the original one and its first offspring pair, are in the cage. Now, during the third month, only the original pair generates another new pair. The first offspring pair must wait a month before it becomes productive. So at the end of the third month, there are 3 pairs in total in the cage – the initial pair and the two offspring pairs that the original pair has thus far produced. If we keep tabs on the situation month by month, we can show the sequence of pairs that the cage successively contains as follows: 1, 1, 2, 3. The first digit represents the number of pairs in the cage at the start; the second, the number after one month; the third, the number after two months; and the fourth, the number after three months.

During the fourth month, the original pair produces yet another pair. At that point the first offspring pair produces its own offspring pair. The second pair produced by the original rabbits has not yet started producing. Therefore, during that month, a total of 2 newborn pairs of rabbits are added to the cage. Altogether, at the end of the month there are the previous 3 pairs plus the 2 newborn ones, making a total of 5 pairs in the cage. This number can now be added to our sequence: 1, 1, 2, 3, 5. During the fifth month, the original pair produces yet another newborn pair; the first offspring pair (now fully productive) produces another pair of its own as well; and now the second offspring pair produces its own first pair. The other rabbit pairs in the cage have not started producing offspring yet. So at the end of the fifth month, 3 newborn pairs have been added to the 5 pairs that were previously in the cage, making the total number of pairs in it 5 + 3 = 8. We can now add this number to our sequence: 1, 1, 2, 3, 5, 8. Continuing to reason in this way, it can be shown that after twelve months, there are 233 pairs in the cage. Now, the intriguing thing about this puzzle is the sequence of pairs itself, on a month-by-month basis:

$$1, 1, 2, 3, 5, 8, 13, 21, 34, 55, 89, 144, 233$$

The salient characteristic of this sequence is that each number in it is the sum of the previous two: for example, 2 (the third number) = 1 + 1 (the sum of the previous two); 3 (the fourth number) = 1 + 2 (the sum of the previous two); and so on. This pattern can of course be extended ad infinitum by applying the simple rule of continually adding the two previous numbers to generate the next:

1, 1, 2, 3, 5, 8, 13, 21, 34, 55, 89, 144, 233, 377, 610, 987, ...

Little did Fibonacci realize how significant his sequence would become. Over the years, the properties of the Fibonacci numbers have been extensively studied, resulting in a considerable literature. The basic pattern hidden in the sequence was studied first by the French-born mathematician Albert Girard (c. 1595–c. 1632). It is expressed as $F_n = F_{n-2} + F_{n-1}$ where F_n stands for any number in the sequence and F_{n-1} the number before it and F_{n-2} the number before F_{n-1}. In 1753 the Scottish mathematician Robert Simson (1687–1768) noted that as the numbers increased in magnitude, the ratio between succeeding numbers approached the *golden ratio*, whose value is .618. The golden ratio results from dividing a segment into two parts in mean and extreme proportion, so that the smaller part is to the larger part as the larger is to the entire segment. For example, if we take the stretch of numbers in the Fibonacci sequence starting with 5 and ending with 34, and then take successive ratios, the results are as follows:

$$3/5 \quad = .6$$
$$5/8 \quad = .625$$
$$8/13 = .615$$
$$13/21 = .619$$
$$21/34 = .617$$

The golden ratio has been found to produce an aesthetic effect – a rectangle the sides of which are in the ratio tends to be perceived as the most pleasing of all rectangles. The question arising from this is obvious: Why would there be a connection between a sequence of numbers produced by a puzzle about copulating rabbits and one of the most enigmatic ratios in the history of human civilization? After all, the puzzle is nothing but a simple representation. The plot thickens, so to speak. In the nineteenth century the term *Fibonacci sequence* was coined by the French mathematician Edouard Lucas, as mentioned, and mathematicians from many domains of inquiry began to discover myriads of patterns hidden within it. Not only that, but stretches of the sequence started cropping up in nature – in the spirals of sunflower heads, in pine cones, in the regular descent (genealogy) of the male bee, in the logarithmic (equiangular) spiral in snail shells, in the arrangement of leaf buds on a stem, in animal horns, in the botanical phenomenon known as phyllotaxis, which relates to the arrangement of the whorls on a pinecone or pineapple, of the petals on a sunflower, of the branches of some stems, and so forth. In most flowers, for example, the number of petals is one of 3, 5, 8, 13, 21, 34, 55, or 89 (lilies have 3 petals, buttercups 5, delphiniums 8, marigolds 13, asters 21, daisies 34 or 55 or 89). The little florets that become seeds in the head of a sunflower are arranged in two sets of spirals: one winding in a clockwise direction, the other counterclockwise. The numbers in the spirals are often (clockwise) 21 and 34, and (counterclockwise) 34 and 55, sometimes 55 and 89, sometimes 89 and 144.

The list of such reifications is truly astounding – so much so that a journal called *The Fibonacci Quarterly* was established in 1963 to publish new discoveries. Why would the solution to a simple puzzle produce numbers that are interconnected with patterns in nature and human life? There is, to the best of my knowledge, no definitive answer to this question. Perhaps representation is, after all, a discovery tool placed in us by nature that allows us to come to grips with reality on our own terms. At the same time, it uncovers things about reality that would otherwise remain hidden. As mathematician Ian Stewart puts it: 'Simple puzzles could open up the hidden depths of the universe.'[7] As a representamen, the Fibonacci sequence seems to have led to an incredible discovery – namely, that a simple recursive pattern constitutes the fabric of a large part of nature.

The predictive power of representation generally lies, arguably, in the fact that it is an imaginative 'modelling strategy.' Representation leads to knowledge not because it is designed as 'knowledge productive' but because it is an imaginative model of something. The power of scientific representation, from geometry to quantum physics, suggests that we are probably 'programmed' to discover things, as mainstream structuralists have always maintained. In observing and representing the facts of existence, thus giving them form, we constantly stumble across hidden patterns. The Fibonacci Puzzle episode brings this out perfectly. In the original tale from which the concept of serendipity is derived, the three princes made their deductions by noticing anomalies that suggested explanations. These spurred their insights. Perhaps Fibonacci saw something in a rabbit pen that tickled his fancy and spurred his insight, and this led to his puzzle and to the hidden reifications it contains. Whatever the truth, Fibonacci's puzzle continues to reverberate with implications for the study of the relation between representation and reality.

But then another question comes to mind: Why should this relationship between mathematical models and physical reality exist unless there is some mysterious underlying connection – a kind of continuity between mind matter and physical matter? And even more mysteriously, is it possible to discover the larger pattern from which the fabric of both these forms of reality has been cut to produce a 'broader picture' of the universe? It is, after all, this desire to see the broader picture that the reifications of the Fibonacci sequence stimulate in us. But it is an elusive picture, and we seem destined never to see it entirely only tantalizing representational glimpses of it here and there.

6.5 Further Reading and Online Resources

Further Reading

Barthes, Roland. *Mythologies*. Paris: Seuil, 1957.
Baudrillard, Jean. *The Mirror of Production*. St Louis, MO: Telos Press, 1988.
– *Toward a Critique of the Political Economy of the Sign*. St Louis, MO: Telos Press, 1978.
Cawelti, John G. *The Six-Gun Mystique*. Bowling Green, OH: Bowling Green State University Popular Press, 1984.
Eco, Umberto. *The Limits of Interpretation*. Bloomington: Indiana University Press, 1990.
merrell, floyd. *Peirce, Signs, and Meaning*. Toronto: University of Toronto Press, 1977.

Online Resources

The Text Semiotics site (www.text-semiotics.org/english4.html) suggested in the previous chapter also has links to relevant sites in representation theory.

7 Applications

There does not exist a category of science to which one can give the name applied science. There are science and the applications of science, bound together as the fruit of the tree which bears it.

Louis Pasteur (1822–95)

7.1 Introduction

Undoubtedly, the strongest appeal of semiotic theory is the many potential applications that it has for the study of cultural systems, spectacles, rituals, artifacts, and the like. Since all of these are sign based, it is obvious that the use of the semiotic notions discussed in this book can be applied to the study of everything from mathematical texts and philosophical concepts to TV sitcoms and blockbuster movies. The purpose of this chapter is to show how semiotics can, in fact, be easily applied to one area: the study of material culture, as it is called in anthropology – that is, of how things such as clothes and food constitute sign systems. There are, of course, many other areas of application; but for the purposes of this book these two will suffice to bring out the essence of what semiotic analysis is all about.

The study of material culture from the semiotic perspective involves, basically, asking how objects, being signs, generate meanings. Needless to say, there is much leeway in how semiotic analysis is conducted, leaving much interpretive space for the analyst in which to move. Overall, though, semioticians attempt to answer three basic questions about some cultural product: What does it mean? How does it encode its meaning(s)? And why does it mean what it means? The first question involves charting the various uses and functions of a sign or text. In some cases, as discussed for the V-sign (§1.1), the meanings are provided by cultural context and, as in anthropological field-work methodology, by asking people appropriate questions. The second question involves utilizing basic sign theory to describe the structural features of the sign or text (iconicity, indexicality, etc.). In the case of the V-sign, it would appear that iconicity played a key role initially – for example, in the meaning 'victory,' it stands for the first letter of the English word; and in its meaning as a feminine symbol it undoubtedly stands for the 'vessel' symbolism associated with female sexuality. Finally, studying why a sign or text means what it means invariably involves the following two forms of analysis:

- *Historical inquiry.* Cultural products must first be examined historically. The reason for this is fairly obvious – to gain any true understanding of what something means, it is necessary to unravel how it came into existence in the first place, to what code it belongs, and how it has been represented.
- *Connotative analysis.* Figuring out what something means culturally means delving into its connotations.

In the case of the V-sign, we found that its various connotations were tied to several historical events and traditions. For example, its use as a sign for 'peace' was a denouncement of its previous meaning of 'victory,' and its use as a symbol of femininity reaches back into symbolic history, in that it is an archetypal counterpart to the phallus.

7.2 Clothing

Clothes are used all over the world not only for protection and modesty, but also for the purpose of constructing socially meaningful messages. Also, some people wear clothes to make ideological, political, and other kinds of socially relevant statements. Clothes, then, constitute a non-verbal sign system and thus are of obvious relevance to semiotic inquiry, in that they reveal how connotation operates in one specific domain of material culture.

What do clothes mean (= the first question of semiotic inquiry)? As with any other object or artefact, we interpret clothes as signs; they stand for such things as the personality, social status, and overall character of the wearer. In effect, clothes mean a vast array of things, depending on social context and function. As such, clothes belong to various *dress codes* that cohere socially to provide information on how to dress for specific occasions. In the semiosphere, clothing is more than just bodily covering for protection. It is a sign system that is interconnected with the other social codes of a society through which social variables such as attitudes, gender, age, class status, and political beliefs can be encoded. This is why uniforms are required by special groups like sports teams, military organizations, and religious institutions. These encode specific kinds of meanings in socially meaningful ways. It is interesting that dress codes, like other types of codes, can be used to lie about oneself: con artists and criminals can dress in three-piece suits to look trustworthy; a crook can dress like a police officer to gain a victim's confidence, and so on. To discourage people from deceiving others through clothing, some societies have even enacted laws that prohibit misleading dressing, defining strictly who can dress in certain ways. In ancient Rome, for instance, only aristocrats were allowed to wear purple-coloured clothes (hence the phrase 'born to the purple'); and in many religiously oriented cultures, differentiated dress codes for men and women are regularly enforced.

To get a true sense of how specific types of clothing mean what they mean (= the second question of semiotic inquiry), it is essential to examine the connection between clothes and the body in a specific cultural context. Across the world, people do not perceive bodies merely as biological structures; they perceive them also as connected to selfhood, and they interpret them as well in culturally specific ways. The human body has been subjected to varying interpretations across history and across cultures. In Ancient Greece, for example, the body was glorified as a source of pleasure; in Imperial Rome, in contrast, it was viewed as a source of moral corruption. The Christian Church has always played on the duality of the body as a temple and as an enemy of the spirit. Because clothes are worn on bodies, they are perceived as extensions of bodily structures and forms with their attendant meanings. When a young Zulu woman is betrothed, she is expected to make a beaded necklace resembling a close-fitting collar with a flat panel attached, which she then gives to her fiancé. Depending on the combination of colours and the bead pattern, the necklace will convey a specific type of romantic message. For example, a combination of pink and white beads in a certain pattern would convey the message 'You are poor, but I want you just the same.'[1]

The human being is the only animal that does not 'go nude,' so to speak, without social repercussions (unless, of course, the social ambiance is that of a nudist camp). Nudity is the oppositional counterpart to clothing. In other words, clothing and nudity constitute a single system of meaning. Acts of 'clothing removal,' such as striptease performances, have appeal arguably because of this unconscious opposition. In an audience setting these have, first and foremost, something of a pagan ritualistic quality to them, based on mimetic portrayals of sexual activities and sexual emotions. As psychoanalysts have suggested, clothing the body has, paradoxically, stimulated curiosity and desire in the body. In a word, what makes nudity appealing in such situations is the absence of clothing. This is also why certain types of clothing, such as shoes, are perceived to have sexual significance. They allude to body parts that have become desirable.

The nude body is itself a sign. This is why visual artists have always had a fascination with the nude figure. The Ancient Greek and Imperial Roman nude statues of male warriors, Michelangelo's (1475–1564) powerful *David* sculpture, and Rodin's (1840–1917) nude sculpture *The Thinker* are all suggestive of the potency of the male body. This 'iconography' of nudity is what enhances the attractiveness of the male in our society. A male with a 'weakling' body is hardly ever perceived as sexually attractive. On the other side of this semiotic paradigm, paintings and sculptures of female nude figures have tended to portray the female body ambiguously as either (1) soft and submissive, as can be seen in the famous Ancient Greek statue the *Venus de Milo*, which represents Aphrodite, the Greek goddess of love and beauty (Venus in Roman mythology); or (2) feral and powerful (as can be seen in the sculptures of Diana in Greek mythology). It is (2) that came to the forefront again in the 1990s. Known as the 'girl power' movement, representations of women in pop culture now emphasize the second of the two iconographic traditions, although (1) has hardly disappeared.

The interplay between clothing and nudity as oppositional values in sign systems is part of a culture's historical iconography. This iconography, which is largely unconscious, conditions representations of bodies in virtually all areas of human social life, from advertising and erotica to religious dress.

Why do clothes mean what they mean (= the third question of semiotic inquiry)? No one knows exactly why or when people first wore clothes. Estimates trace the origin of clothing back 100,000 years. Archaeological research suggests that prehistoric hunters may have worn the skins of bears or reindeer in order to keep warm or as a sign of personal skill, bravery, and strength. By the end of the Old Stone Age – about 25,000 years ago – people had invented the needle, which enabled them to sew skins together. They had also learned to make yarn from the thread-like parts of some plants or from the fur or hair of some animals. In addition, they had learned to weave yarn into cloth. At the same time, people had begun to raise plants, which gave them a steady supply of materials for making yarn. They had also started to herd sheep and other wool-producing animals.

At a biological level, clothes have a very important function indeed – they enhance survival considerably. This is the level of denotation in semiotic theory – the level at which a referent is tied to biological or practical needs (§1.3). Clothes are, denotatively, human-made extensions of the body's protective resources, perceived as additions to our protective bodily hair and skin thickness. This is why clothing styles vary with geography and climate. But the denotative biological function of clothes is hardly what clothing is perceived to be all about in the semiosphere, where clothes take on a whole range of connotations that have little to do with survival. These have accrued over time, leading to the formation of dress codes that inform people how to clothe themselves in social situations. To someone who knows nothing about Amish culture, the blue or charcoal *Mutze* of the Amish male is just a jacket. But to the Amish, the blue *Mutze* signals that the wearer is between sixteen and thirty-five years of age, the charcoal one that he is over thirty-five. Similarly, to an outsider the Russian *kalbak* appears to be a brimless red hat. To a rural Russian, however, it means that the wearer is a medical doctor. Even in cold climates, some people seem more interested in decorating their bodies than in protecting them. In the 1830s the British biologist Charles Darwin (1809–82) travelled to the island of Tierra del Fuego off the southern tip of South America. There he saw people who wore only a little paint and a small cloak made of animal skin, in spite of the cold rain and the sleet. Darwin gave the people scarlet cloth; they took it and wrapped it around their necks, instead of wearing it around the lower body for warmth. Despite the cold weather, the people wore clothing not for protective reasons, but primarily for decorating their bodies and making them appear attractive.

In traditional tribal and religious cultures, dress codes rarely change and are enforced to preserve cultural continuity and values. Shamans, for example, have always worn special clothing to identify themselves.

This continues to be so for all kinds of clerics today. Non-religious groups approach clothes with the same mentality. Motorcycle gang members, for instance, wear leather jackets, boots, and various items such as brass knuckles to convey toughness and group identity. In effect, dress characterizes group membership and beliefs. This is why many religious groups believe it is wrong to care about wearing clothes as fashion. They believe that people should be concerned with other matters. The Amish – to cite just one example – have this kind of belief system. Amish men wear plain, dark clothes, and Amish women wear long, plain dresses.

However, in some cultures – such as the American one – clothing trends are in constant flux, reflecting social trends and political movements. In such cultures, *fashion* is an important feature of daily life. Take the case of women wearing pants in Western (and other) cultures. Young women started wearing pants in the 1930s and 1940s, but did so sporadically. Denotatively and connotatively, the one who 'wore the pants' in a family was a male. With the change in social role structures during the 1950s and 1960s, women began to wear pants regularly and sending out the new social messages that this entailed. Feminism was symbolized largely by women wearing pants. In the 1960s, gender equality was symbolized by unisex fashion, emblemized by the wearing of jeans by both males and females. This dress code gave material substance to feminism and to the social ideology that it was constructing. The reverse situation, incidentally, has not as yet transpired. Except in special ritualistic circumstances – for example, the wearing of a Scottish kilt – Western men have never worn skirts. When they do, it is typically labelled an act of 'transvestitism.'

Fashion trends can often be seen in the wearing of certain items of dress, which take on special meanings. For example, the meanings of headgear vary widely, depending not only on climate but also on customs. Thus, a Russian farmer wears a fur hat to protect himself from the cold; a South American cowboy wears a felt gaucho hat as part of his traditional costume; the American cowboy wears a wide-brimmed hat for protection from the sun; the members of a nation's armed services wear a hat as part of their uniform; the hats of coal miners, fire fighters, and matadors indicate the wearer's occupation; clowns wear colourful, ridiculous hats to express fun and happiness; and the list could go on and on. But outside of these traditional contexts, hats have tended to take on 'fashion value' throughout the Western world, resulting in the wearing of many kinds of unusual hats. During the 1400s, European women wore a tall, cone-shaped hat called a *hennin* as part of fashion. This hat measured from 0.9 to 1.2 metres high and had a long, floating veil. The Gainsborough hat became a popular fashion item for both men and women in the late 1700s. It had a wide brim and was decorated with feathers and ribbons. Today, people wear a hat that they believe makes them look attractive or that identifies them as part of some group (e.g., an adolescent clique). This is why much protective headgear today, such as fur hoods and rain hats, is both attractive and stylish. Even the caps of police officers and military personnel are designed to improve the wearer's appearance.

Until the Renaissance, fashion was largely the privilege of the rich and powerful. Since the early decades of the twentieth century, however, it has become an intrinsic component of the lifestyle of common people in many parts of the world. Fashion statement has become personal statement, not just an acknowledgment of one's social role and importance.

Fashion can thus be defined as the prevailing style or custom of dress. As mentioned several times earlier, although fashion usually refers to dress, it does not mean the same thing as clothing. People have always worn clothes that reflect the long-standing customs of their communities, and clothing styles changed extremely slowly in the past. Fashion, however, causes styles to change rapidly for a variety of historical, psychological, and sociological reasons. A clothing style may be introduced as a fashion; that style then becomes a custom if it is handed down from generation to generation. A fashion that quickly comes and goes is called a fad.[2] To understand how fashion codes emerge, it is instructive to consider the history of the male business suit, which is still worn in offices across the Western world, in its bare essentials. The subtext underlying the apparel text is, of course, *dress for success*. How did this subtext crystallize?

The starting point for answering this question is seventeenth-century England, when a bitter conflict in social ideology arose between two segments of society: the Royalist 'Cavaliers,' who were faithful to King Charles I, and the Puritans, who were followers of Oliver Cromwell (1599–1658), the military, political, and religious figure who led the Parliamentarians to victory in the English Civil War (1642–49). This conflict was a battle of lifestyles, with the two warring camps seeking to gain political, religious, and cultural control of English society. The Cavaliers were aristocrats who only superficially followed the teachings of the Anglican Church. Their main penchant was for a life of indulgence (at least as the Puritans perceived it). They wore colourful clothes, flamboyant feathered hats, beards, and long flowing hair. This image of the Cavalier as a 'swashbuckler' has been immortalized by literary works such as *The Three Musketeers* by Alexandre Dumas (1802–70), and *Cyrano de Bergerac* by Edmond Rostand (1868–1918). The Puritans, on the other hand, frowned on this type of fashion, which to them represented a 'degenerate lifestyle.' Cromwell's followers, known as the 'Roundheads,' cropped their hair very short, forbade all carnal pleasures, and prohibited the wearing of frivolous clothing. They wore dark suits and dresses with white shirts and collars. Their clothes conveyed sobriety, plainness, and rigid moralism.

The Cavaliers were in power throughout the 1620s and the 1630s. During this period the Puritans escaped from England and immigrated to America, bringing with them their lifestyle, rigid codes of conduct, and clothing styles. In 1645 the Puritans, led by Cromwell, defeated the Royalist forces and executed the king. Subsequently, many Cavaliers also immigrated to America. Since the Puritans had already established colonies in the northeast, the Cavaliers decided to set up colonies in the south. The king's son, Charles II, escaped to France to set up a court in exile. For a decade, England was ruled by the Puritans. Frowning on all sorts of pleasure-seeking recreations, they closed down theatres, censored books, enforced Sunday laws, and forbade the wearing of flashy clothing.

Soon after Cromwell's death in 1658, the Puritans were thrown out of power; in 1660, England welcomed back the exiled king, Charles II. The following twenty-five years, known as the Restoration, saw a return to the lifestyle and fashions of the Cavaliers. For the next two centuries the Puritans bided their time. They were excluded from holding political office, from attending university, and from engaging in socially vital enterprises. Nevertheless, over the years they maintained their severe lifestyle and dress codes.

Then came the Industrial Revolution, and the Puritans had their final and lasting revenge. Their lifestyle – based on thrift, diligence, temperance, and industriousness, which some have called the 'Protestant work ethic' – allowed them to take advantage of the economic conditions in the new industrialized world. In both America and England, Cromwell's descendants became rich and eventually took over the reigns of economic power. Ever since, Puritan ethics and fashion in the workforce have influenced British and North American business culture, not to mention social mores and values at large. The origins of modern corporate capitalism are to be found in those values. The belief that hard work and 'clean living' are necessarily interrelated and that this combination leads to wealth and prosperity had become widespread by the turn of the last century. To this day, there is a deeply felt conviction in capitalist culture that hard work and strict living codes will lead to success both in this life and in the afterlife.

The business suit is a contemporary version of Puritan dress. The toned down colours (blues, browns, greys) that the business world demands are the contemporary reflexes of the Puritan's fear and dislike of colour and ornament. During the 'hippie' decades of the 1960s and early 1970s, the office scene came briefly under the influence of a new form of Cavalierism, with the wearing of colourful suits, turtleneck sweaters rather than white shirts, longer hair, sideburns, Nehru jackets, medallions, and beards. This new 'fashion dare' made a serious attempt to take over the world of corporate capitalism. But it was bound to fail, and the hippie movement of the 1960s was defeated by conservative neopuritanical forces in the late 1970s and 1980s. Once again the 'business suit' model became the dress code for all of corporate North America, with only minor variations in detail.

The business suit somehow endures, perhaps because it is intrinsically intertwined with the history of capitalism. But nowadays, even this fashion code has become rather eclectic, not to say fragmented. Take, for example, the length of the skirt in the female business suit code. Mini, maxi, and normal length skirts are alternatively in and out of fashion. Evidently, a detail such as length of skirt is in itself meaningless. What appears to count is what it implies as a signifier about the ever-fluctuating perceptions of women in the workplace and in society at large. When the mini is 'in,' it perhaps implies an increased emphasis on sexual freedom in the culture. When it is 'out,' it perhaps implies the opposite – a decreased emphasis on sexuality. Whatever the case, the point here is that the specific elements and features of a fashion code invariably have a connotative value derived from the culture's broader social codes.

True fashions first appeared in northern Europe and Italy in the Late Middle Ages with the rise of the bourgeois class, when a system of social classes developed. At this time, Europeans began to classify one another into groups based on such factors as wealth, ancestry, and occupation. The clothes that people wore helped identify them as members of a particular social class. Before the Late Middle Ages, only wealthy and powerful individuals concerned themselves with the style of their clothes. But when the class system developed, the general population began to compete for positions within society. Fashion was one means by which people did this. One of the first true fashions appeared among young bourgeois Italian men during the Renaissance. While their elders dressed in long traditional robes, the young males wore tights and short, close-fitting jackets called doublets. This was one of the first examples of youth-based clothing that intentionally set itself apart from the adult dress code. German soldiers set another early fashion when they slashed their luxurious silk clothes with knives to reveal another colourful garment underneath. Theirs too was a youth-based fashion trend, probably intended to influence their appeal to the opposite sex.

Before the 1800s, many countries controlled fashion with regulations called sumptuary laws. These limited the amount of money people could spend on private luxuries, and were obviously designed to preserve divisions among the classes. In this way, fashion was regulated according to a person's rank in society. In some countries only the ruling class could legally wear silk, fur, and the colours red and purple. In Paris in the 1300s, middle-class women were forbidden by law to wear high headdresses, wide sleeves, and fur trimmings. Other sumptuary laws required people to buy products manufactured in their own country to help the country's economy. For example, an English law in the 1700s prohibited people of all classes from wearing cotton cloth produced outside of England. But the lure of fashion caused many people to break this law. The cloth was so popular that people risked arrest to wear it.

Ordinary people have always hoped to raise their social position by following the fashions of privileged people. Fashions have also emerged to accompany differing perceptions of gender. Until the late 1700s, upper-class European men dressed as elaborately as women did. It was acceptable for men to wear bright-coloured or pastel suits trimmed with gold and lace, hats decorated with feathers, high-heeled shoes, and fancy jewellery. But by the mid-1800s, men had abandoned such flamboyance in favour of plain, dark-coloured wool suits. Society came to view this new fashion style as democratic, businesslike, and masculine. Until the early 1900s, European and American women rarely wore trousers, and their skirts almost always covered their ankles. By the 1920s, however, standards of feminine modesty had changed to the point that women began to wear both trousers and shorter skirts.

Contrary to popular belief, political events seldom cause fashions to change. However, political events do sometimes speed up changes that have already begun, as we saw in the case of the business suit. For example, during the French Revolution (1789–99), simple clothing replaced the extravagant costumes made fashionable by French aristocrats. But simple styles had become popular years earlier, when men in England started wearing practical, dark suits instead of elegant, colourful clothes. English people identified these plain suits with political and personal liberty. Because many French people admired English liberty, this style was already becoming fashionable in France before the revolution.

In the nineteenth century, the invention of mechanical looms, chemical dyes, artificial fabrics, and methods of mass production made fashions affordable to many more people. In addition, new means of mass communication spread European and American fashions throughout the rest of the world. The Industrial Revolution created a 'fashion global village.' Since then, fashion shows and fashion magazines have proliferated. And, as Barthes pointed out, they change constantly because rapid turnover guarantees economic success. It is the only constant in contemporary fashion trends.

Today, it is attractive-looking celebrities rather than aristocrats who set trends. People tend to follow fashion primarily to make themselves similarly attractive. When the standard of beauty changes, fashion changes with it. For example, when physical fitness became a popular standard of good looks in the 1980s, people began to wear exercise and athletic clothing more often. A clothing style may become fashionable over time with many different groups. People began wearing blue jeans during the mid-1800s as ordinary work clothes. For decades, they were worn chiefly by outdoor labourers such as farmers and cowboys. In the 1940s and 1950s, American teenagers adopted blue jeans as a comfortable, casual youth fashion. Young people during the 1960s wore blue jeans as a symbol of rebellious political and social beliefs. By the 1970s, people no longer considered jeans symbols of youth or of rebellion, and expensive designer jeans had become fashionable.

7.3 Food

Food, like clothing, is perceived throughout the world not only as organic material for biological support or sustenance, but also as a means of constructing socially relevant messages. Edibility, moreover, is largely governed by the historical meanings imprinted in specific foods. The central concept sustaining semiotic research in this area is that foods constitute signs that are marked for various social meanings.

What do foods mean (= the first question of semiotic inquiry)? In cultural settings, different types of food, culinary preparations, eating events and rituals, and food-celebrating occasions have specific meanings. The eating of meat, for example, is dependent on the specific connotations that a certain animal has in a cultural setting. In Western society, eating beef is a common occurrence, no matter what form its preparation takes (steak, hamburger, etc.), because cattle meat is perceived as an edible food; whereas the eating of rabbit or cat meat is not, because these animals are defined culturally as domestic companions. As this simple illustration indicates, meat is a sign that derives its meanings from the network of culture-specific meanings that animals possess. In most meat-eating societies, certain animals are identified as sources of food, and others are not, rendering them 'uneatable.'

Food is, clearly, much more than substance for nourishment and sustenance. So how does it take on meaning (= the second question of semiotic inquiry)? Food takes on meaning when it is cooked, and the ways in which it is cooked bring out the various connotations it has. In 1964, Claude Lévi-Strauss argued that the difference between 'raw' and 'cooked' food lies at the foundation of religious and social practices.[3] Many Christians, for instance, say grace before starting a cooked meal together; and Jews say special prayers before partaking of wine and bread. At a formal meal, the order in which dishes are presented, what combinations can be served in tandem, how the foods are to be placed on the table, who has preference in being served, who must show deference, who does the speaking and who the listening, who sits where, and what topics of conversation are appropriate are all based on traditions derived from cooking food. All cultures, moreover, have a discrete set of table rituals and manners accompanying the cooking of food that are inculcated into the members of the culture from birth. If you do not know the code of table manners, you will have to learn it in order to continue living in the culture without censure and disapprobation.

The social importance of food was noted first in writing by the Greek historian Herodotus (c. 484–425 BCE), who spent a large part of his life travelling through Asia, Babylon, Egypt, and Greece, noting and recording for posterity the differences he perceived (with respect to Athenian culture) in the language, dress, food, etiquette, legends, and rituals of the different peoples he came across. The annotations he made constitute the first significant accounts of the cultures of virtually the entire ancient Middle East, including those of the Scythians, Medes, Persians, Assyrians, and Egyptians. Inspired by Herodotus, other ancient historians also made it a point to describe systematically and comparatively the languages, character, manners, and geographical distribution of the peoples they visited. As these ancient 'anthropologists' discovered, in a social ambiance food takes on a significance that transcends its basic survival function, and this affects perceptions of its edibility. Food mirrors social organization, religious beliefs, and other aspects of communal life. It is, in other words, an important element for understanding the overall 'code' of a culture.

Systems of *etiquette*, incidentally, existed even in early tribal settings. As prehistoric people began to interact with one another, they learned to behave in ways that made life easier and more pleasant. For example, as people learned to plant crops and farm, the ability to store food led to communal eating. Rituals developed for the preparation and sharing of meals, and these over time evolved into the table manners of today. Later, early civilizations such as those of Ancient Greece and Imperial Rome developed rules for proper social conduct. Such rules became more formal in the Middle Ages, during which boys training to become knights learned a code of conduct called *chivalry*. According to this code, a knight was to devote himself to the Christian church and his country and to treat women with great respect. Some aspects of chivalry – particularly the special treatment of women – became a traditional part of manners.

Much of today's formal etiquette originated in the French royal courts during the 1600s and 1700s. King Louis XIV drew up a daily list of events, giving time, place, and proper dress. This was posted in his palace at Versailles as an *etiquette*, a French word meaning ticket, to help the nobles know what to do. It brought order to court society, and other monarchs adopted the code of behaviour for their own courts. Over time, the upper classes throughout the Western world adopted the code.

Why does food have so many meanings (= the third question of semiotic inquiry)? It goes without saying that survival without food is impossible. So, denotatively, food can be defined as 'survival substance.' Yet, as already discussed, in the semiosphere, food and eating involve culture-specific connotations. A term often used to designate the system of connotations that food evokes is *cuisine*. Cuisine tells us not only what certain people eat but also how they prepare it, and ultimately it reveals a lot about them.

The earliest people probably ate whatever plant food they could find, including wild fruits, mushrooms, nuts, roots, and seeds. They also caught fish and small land animals and ate the meat of the dead animals they found. Over time, they developed weapons to hunt large animals and probably spent much time searching for them. If the food supply in an area ran out, they apparently moved on. They roasted some of their food over burning wood from fires that started naturally. After they discovered how to make fire, they started roasting food more often. After they learned how to make pots, they began boiling and stewing food.

Around 8000 BCE, people began raising plants and animals for food – hence the rise of farming as a communal activity, assuring people of a steadier food supply. Agriculture also encouraged people to settle in one area instead of travelling about in search of food. Grains were especially important crops for the early farming communities. Also important was the raising of cattle, goats, sheep, and other animals for meat and milk. Some prehistoric groups were nomadic. They travelled across the countryside in patterns, raising such animals as camels, goats, and sheep. Between 3500 and 1500 BCE, the first great civilizations developed in river valleys, such as the Nile Valley in Egypt, the Tigris–Euphrates Valley in what is now Iraq, the Indus Valley in what are now Pakistan and Northwest India, and the Huang He Valley in China. All of these valleys had fertile soil and a favourable climate, which enabled farmers to produce abundant yields. In ancient Egypt, for example, farmers along the Nile could raise two or three crops a year on the same fields. They grew barley and wheat as well as vegetables such as beans, lettuce, and peas. The Egyptians also cultivated fruits such as grapes and melons. Their livestock included cattle, goats, and sheep.

At first, the Ancient Greek and Imperial Roman societies could not produce enough food for their growing populations. They thus needed to import large quantities of food from other countries. This may be why both civilizations set out to conquer and colonize lands that had plentiful food supplies. By the third century CE, the Roman Empire covered much of Europe, most of the Middle East, and the Mediterranean coast of Africa. The empire's large farms specialized in raising wheat, which formed the basis of the Roman diet.

Human culture is, arguably, the consequence of efforts to secure a stable source of food and to invent a technology to make food abundant and durable. As mentioned earlier, the anthropologist Claude Lévi-Strauss argued that the origin of culture can in fact be traced to the advent of 'cooking technology.' He argued that this transformation was accomplished by two processes – roasting and boiling, both of which were among the first significant technological advances made by humanity. Roasting is more primitive than boiling in that it calls for direct contact between the food and a fire. Boiling involves more advanced technology, in that the process is mediated by a pot. It was boiling that led to the institution of true culture, which implies the sharing of food in a community of others. At that point food took on symbolic meanings.

To grasp how this may have come about, it is useful to imagine being in a 'Robinson Crusoe' situation – Robinson Crusoe being the protagonist in the Daniel Defoe's (c. 1660–1731) famous novel *The Life and Adventures of Robinson Crusoe*, which appeared in 1719. This book is fiction; however, it is based on the real adventures of a seaman, Alexander Selkirk (1676–1721), who was marooned on an island off the coast of Chile. The novel chronicles Crusoe's ingenious attempts to overcome the hardships he faces on the island. Imagine being abandoned on an isolated island in the middle of nowhere like Crusoe was. When we lose the support and security of a social ambiance, our first instincts are to survive in any way we can. In such a situation, the need for food and water takes precedence over all else, and we are hardly likely to be fussy about what we eat. Basically, we will eat whatever we find.

Now, suppose that after living alone on the island for a few years we discover other similarly abandoned individuals, each on some remote part of the island, but all of whom speak the same language. Since there is strength in numbers, the decision is made by all concerned to become a group; within that group, specific roles are assigned to each individual for the procurement, storage, and preparation of food. This division of labour constitutes an emergent 'social contract.' As time passes, other social contracts are made, all designed to ensure survival. The food eaten and its method of preparation will start at that point in time to take on meanings that transcend survival. The group may want, for instance, to reserve a day of the week to eat a special type of food, cooked in a special way, to symbolize the gratitude each one feels (for having survived). From this a rudimentary religious tradition can be established. Other traditions can be similarly instituted.

This vignette suggests that food cooked for a community of eaters is bound to take on significance beyond that of a survival substance. When especially abundant food sources became available, early humans settled in permanent, year-round communities, where they learned to domesticate plants and animals for food, transportation, clothing, and so on. With greater population concentrations and permanent living sites, social contracts evolved into cultural institutions complete with religious ceremonies and ritualistic food events (such as communal meals and feasts). These early hunting–gathering societies soon developed complex belief systems regarding the supernatural world and the behaviours of spirits and gods. Food became a part of ritual and communal meaning-sharing, and was often offered to the deities in return for specific favours. To this day, food is perceived invariably as a key constituent of all kinds of ceremonies and rituals, from feasts (weddings, bar and bat mitzvahs, etc.) to simple social gatherings. We schedule 'breakfast,' 'lunch,' and 'dinner' events on a daily basis. Indeed, we plan our days around meals. Even a common romantic date is almost unthinkable without some eating component (ranging from the popcorn eaten at a movie theatre to an elaborate meal at a trendy restaurant).

During rituals, food items take on specific symbolic meanings. Take, for example, bread. We talk of the *bread of life*, of *earning one's bread*, and so on because bread is a symbol for life (this is so in many cultures). The word *companion*, incidentally, comes from Latin and means literally the person 'with whom we share bread.' This is true even in our own day; we still expect to have bread on hand at every meal. Bread is associated with life probably because it is one of the oldest foods eaten and prepared by humans. Prehistoric people made flat bread by mixing grain meal with water and baking the resulting dough on heated rocks. Historians believe that the Egyptians learned to make yeast bread around 2600 BCE. The Ancient Greeks learned bread making from the Egyptians and later taught the Romans how to do it. By the first century CE the Romans had passed this knowledge on to peoples of the many parts of Europe they had conquered.

Many of food's symbolic meanings derive from accounts of human origins. The biblical story of Adam and Eve, for instance, revolves around the eating of a forbidden fruit. The representation of this fruit as an apple came in medieval pictorial representations of the Eden scene. Since then the Biblical symbolism of the apple as 'forbidden knowledge' continues to resonate in many societies. This is why the apple tree symbolizes the 'tree of knowledge'; why the 'Apple' computer company has probably chosen this fruit for its company name and logo; and so on. The discovery and cultivation of the apple dates back to 6500 BCE in Asia Minor. Ramses II of Egypt cultivated apples in orchards along the Nile in the thirteenth century BCE. The ancient Greeks grew apple trees from the seventh century BCE onwards. They designated the apple 'the golden fruit,' since in Greek mythology the apple was given to Hera from the Garden of the Hesperides as a wedding present when she married Zeus.

As another example of food symbolism, consider lamb meat. This is an especially important Easter food in central and eastern European countries. It is eaten at this time period of the liturgical year because it represents Jesus and relates His death to that of the lamb sacrificed on the first Passover. This is why Christians traditionally refer to Jesus as 'the Lamb of God.' In many homes a lamb-shaped cake decorates the table at Easter. Many Eastern Orthodox Christians hang pictures of the Easter lamb in their homes.

Similar accounts can be sketched for almost any of the traditional foods we eat today. Symbolism is also the reason why the meat of certain animals is not eaten by certain people. And it is also the reason for fasting. Fasting is one of a number of rites in which physical activities are reduced or suspended, resulting in a state of quiescence symbolically comparable to death or to the state preceding birth. Fasts have been part of fertility rites since prehistoric times.

Some fasts are intended to induce fertility, others to avert catastrophe or to serve as penance for sin. The ancient Assyrians and Babylonians observed fasts as a form of penance. Among Jews, too, fasting has always signified penitence and purification. This is why fasting is observed annually on the Day of Atonement, Yom Kippur. The fast observed by Muslims during the month of Ramadan is another expression of atonement. Although most Protestant churches retained fasting after the Reformation in the sixteenth century, stricter Protestants such as the Puritans condemned traditional fasts. The Orthodox Church, on the other hand, continues to observe fasts rigorously. Native North Americans hold tribal fasts to avert impending disasters. And political fasting, known as 'hunger striking,' has been employed as a political weapon ever since Mohandas Gandhi, leader of the struggle for India's freedom, used it effectively in the early and mid-1900s.

The counterpart to fasting is overeating. One tradition based on culinary indulgence is *carnival*, which in Christian cultures consists of feasting and merrymaking just before Lent. The Mardi Gras in New Orleans is a famous carnival, as is the one in Rio de Janeiro. The word is derived from the Italian *carnevale*, which in turn is derived from the Latin *carne*, 'meat' + *levare*, 'to remove.' Thus it means, essentially, 'farewell to meat.' From this religious tradition, the modern concept of a carnival as a form of outdoor amusement consisting of exhibits, games, rides, shows, and all kinds of tempting foods gradually developed.

Eating foods constitutes an act of 'sign eating.' This can be seen when someone is asked to eat something perceived semiotically as inedible. In Anglo-American culture that is the case with rabbits, which are defined by and large as 'household companions' rather than as sources of food, even though there are some notable exceptions to this, especially in rural cuisines. The same culture also does not classify foxes or dogs as edible food items; yet the former is reckoned a delicacy in Russia, and the latter a delicacy in China. On the other hand, bovine meat (beef steaks, hamburgers, etc.), lamb meat, and poultry meat are eaten routinely in Anglo-American and European culture, with few negative perceptions and gustatory reactions. In India, on the other hand, a cow is considered by religious tradition to be sacred and, therefore, beef is perceived to be inedible.

It is interesting that it was the Imperial Romans who domesticated the rabbit, which flourished throughout their empire as a food source. In sixteenth-century England, rabbits were prized instead for their fur. For this reason they were bred selectively in order to improve their coats. In the nineteenth century, England passed strict game laws prohibiting rabbit hunting. In the rest of the one-time Roman Empire, however, the rabbit continued to be viewed as a food source. By the turn of the twentieth century, rabbits had been redefined in Anglo-American culture as household animals. The reinforcement of the anthropomorphic connotations that the rabbit has since taken on can be seen in the popularity of fictional rabbit characters (*Bugs Bunny*, the *Easter Bunny*, *Benjamin Bunny*) that have become a part of childhood.

Edibility is, in sum, more a product of culture than of nature. Some flora and fauna have demonstrably harmful effects on the human organism. Those aside, the list of flora and fauna that are considered to be edible (or inedible) is very much the result of history and tradition. We cannot get nourishment from eating tree bark, grass, or straw. But we certainly could get it from eating frogs, ants, earthworms, silkworms, lizards, and snails. Most people in Anglo-American culture would, however, respond with disgust at the thought of eating such potential food items. Yet there are cultures in which they are eaten not only for nourishment but also as part of symbolic traditions. The expression *to develop a taste* for some 'foreign' food reveals how closely tied edibility is to cultural perception. Left alone on that hypothetical Robinson Crusoe island described above, the question would certainly not be one of 'taste,' but of 'survival' at any taste.

So close is the association between food and culture that the former is used commonly and stereotypically as a template for evaluating other people and their cultures. People perceive gustatory differences in cuisine as fundamental differences in world view and lifestyle – as differences between 'us' and 'them.' It is relevant to note that when people come to accept the cuisine of others not only as tasty but also as a delicacy, the culture of the food makers concomitantly is perceived much more positively.

Food codes, like all other kinds of social codes, are regulatory systems – they control what kinds of food are eaten, when they are eaten, who is allowed to eat them, and so forth. Predictably, these vary considerably from culture to culture, having an effect on how certain foods are perceived, on how they are prepared, on who has priority in eating them, and so on. In some traditional societies, for example, the oldest member of a family eats first, followed by the next generation, on down to the youngest. At matrimonial ceremonies throughout the world, specific kinds of codes may dictate the organization of parts of the ceremony (e.g., the wedding party normally sits apart from the invited guests).

Above all else, food codes dictate how eating events are organized, including the order in which dishes are presented; what combinations can be served in tandem; how the foods are to be placed on the table; who has preference in being served; who must show deference; who does the speaking and who the listening; who sits where; and which topics of conversation are appropriate. Dinner invitations can be fraught with hope and danger, constituting dramatic events at which decisions may be made and important relationships forged or broken.

Eating events are so crucial to the establishment and maintenance of social relations and harmony that virtually every culture assigns an area of the domestic abode to eating functions and ceremonies. All cultures, moreover, have a discrete set of table rituals and manners that are inculcated into the members of the culture from birth. If you do not know the table-manner code of a certain culture, you will have to learn it in order to continue living in that culture without reproach and disapproval. Consider a concrete example. If you have never eaten spaghetti before, if you find yourself in Italy you will have to learn that the 'correct' way to eat it is with a fork. In nineteenth-century Naples, where the modern-day version of this dish comes from, people ate spaghetti with their hands by raising each string of pasta in the hand, throwing back the head, and lowering the string into the mouth without slurping. Today, the correct manner of eating spaghetti is to twirl it around a fork in small doses, then to insert the fork into the mouth. Eating spaghetti in any other way would be perceived as a breach of the relevant table-manner code.

Table-manner codes often involve the use of flatware. Knives, spoons, forks, and other specialized implements for eating and serving food have until recent times been the privilege of the aristocracy. In Egypt, Greece, and Rome, the knives and spoons of the aristocracy were made of precious materials, including silver and gold, and were sometimes decorated. The Romans also possessed skewers. These were forerunners of forks. From the Middle Ages until the Renaissance, the knife remained the principal table utensil. Forks came into common table use in Italy in the 1500s. At the same time, spoons made the transition from kitchen utensils to table flatware. From that time onwards, flatware came to be used by all peoples of all classes. During the nineteenth century, many other items of flatware were created, such as teaspoons, butter knives, and salad forks.

Semioticians typically view food codes as prototypical social codes. The signs that we use to make messages are not randomly chosen. When we enter into an eating event, for example, we will be able to participate successfully in it only if we know the appropriate food code. This code provides information about how to eat food, when to speak during eating, and so on. Food codes tend to be more or less stable, varying little over time if at all. But they are adaptive nonetheless, and like all codes, they are sensitive to context. Eating a wiener with the hands would be inappropriate in a high-class restaurant, but it would be one of the ways to eat it at an open-air meal among friends at a barbecue, where cutlery may not be available. Clearly, the physical context of occurrence and social frame of reference will determine how a food item is eaten. A restaurant, for that matter, is a social code. This is why we interpret anything that is eaten there differently than if it is eaten somewhere else.

7.4 The Quest for Meaning

As the examples of clothing and food show, the basic concepts of semiotic theory provide a concrete framework for understanding social phenomena such as rituals, classification (edible vs non–edible, etc.), fashion trends, and so on. They allow us, in effect, to see a commonality in them that coheres into an overall system of meaning that defines human existence.

As I have attempted to show in this book, mainly through illustration, it is important to the overall study of knowledge to understand signs and how they constitute our knowledge systems. *Homo sapiens* is a sign maker and a sign user. But semiotics also warns us that signs are hardly true tokens of knowledge – they are merely representations of knowledge. A sign selects what is to be known and memorized from the infinite variety of things that are in the world. Although we create new signs to help us gain new knowledge and to modify previous knowledge – that is what artists, scientists, and writers, for instance, are always doing – by and large, we literally let our culture 'do the thinking' for us. We are born into an already fixed system of meaning, called culture, that will largely determine how we view the world around us. Only if, hypothetically, all our knowledge (which is maintained in the form of codes) were somehow erased from the face of the earth would we need to rely once again on our instinctive meaning-making tendencies to represent the world all over again.

As an example, consider the concept of health. Although this might at first appear to capture a universally shared meaning, in actual fact what is considered to be 'naturally healthy' in one culture may not coincide with views of health in another. Health cannot be defined ahistorically, aculturally, or in purely absolute terms. This does not deny the existence of events and states in the body that will lead to disease or illness. All organisms have a species-specific bodily warning system that alerts them to dangerous changes in bodily states. But in the human species, bodily states are interpreted in culture-specific ways. This is why in American culture today a 'healthy body' is considered to be one that is lean and muscular. Conversely, in others it is one that Americans would consider too plump and rotund. A 'healthy lifestyle' might be seen by some cultures to inhere in rigorous physical activity, while in others it might be envisaged as inhering in a more leisurely and sedentary lifestyle.

Moreover, as the late writer Susan Sontag (1933–2004) cogently

argued in her compelling 1978 book *Illness as Metaphor*, culture predis-
poses people to think of specific illnesses in certain ways. Using the
example of cancer, Sontag pointed out that in the not too distant past
the very word *cancer* was said to have killed some patients who would
not have necessarily succumbed to the malignancy from which they
suffered: 'As long as a particular disease is treated as an evil, invinci-
ble predator, not just a disease, most people with cancer will indeed be
demoralized by learning what disease they have.'[4] Sontag's point that
people suffer more from interpreting their disease as a sign than from
the disease itself is, indeed, a well-taken and instructive one.

In an analogous treatment of the concept of disease, Jacalyn Duffin
argues that disease is what we define it to be.[5] She points out that
'lovesickness' was once considered a true disease, even though it originated in the poetry of antiquity. Its demise as a disease is the result of
twentieth-century scepticism. She also argues that Hepatitis C – a
major cause of cirrhosis, which experts think results mainly from using
contaminated needles for injecting illegal drugs, tattooing, or body
piercing – also stems from ancient tradition and that it has crystallized
as a modern disease as a result of discoveries in virology and recent
tragedies in transfusion medicine. At any given point in time, concepts
of disease crystallize from a combination of social, cultural, legal, and
scientific factors, not from any absolutist notion of disease. Similar
arguments can be made for such maladies as acne and depression.
Whether or not they are considered diseases depends on largely cultural factors. Acne is a skin disorder that is associated with modern-
day teenagers; it consists of various kinds of blemishes, mainly on the
face, upper chest, and back. It is not considered a disease, unless of
course it becomes severe. Depression, on the other hand, is now classified as a serious mental disease, in which a person suffers long
periods of sadness and other negative feelings. In the past, such suffering would have been attributed to factors other than those that characterize a physical sickness. Raising it to the status of a disease has,
however, entailed consequences, including pharmacological intervention by doctors.

Signs shape us in every way imaginable. But they do not imprison
us cognitively or creatively. Particular signs influence how we perceive
reality, but they can also be used as 'tools of discovery.' This reveals
that we perhaps use signs as part of a system of awareness of what
reality is all about – a system that is unique to our species. As discussed in the previous chapter, discovery is a sign-based process. And

real discoveries do happen, all the time. In one sense, signs leave a peculiar human imprint on nature. At the same time, they serendipitously unravel patterns within nature itself. The invention of the mathematical ratio π (= approximately 3.14) was motivated by the need to calculate the area of a circle. But as it turns out, this very same ratio appears to be an unexpected 'descriptor' of such physical phenomena as the motion of a pendulum and the vibration of a string. This synergy between signs and reality is remarkable indeed. From the dawn of civilization to the present age, it has always been felt that there is an intrinsic connection between the two.

The raison d'être of semiotics is, arguably, to investigate whether reality can exist independently of the signs that human beings create to represent and think about it. Hopefully, this trek through the basic concepts that make up the science that studies the relation between signs and reality will have been a useful one. A large part of contemporary semiotic work continues to try to explicate the nature of signs, codes, texts, and representation generally. But more and more, semioticians have started searching for the motivations behind semiosis and representational activities. In effect, the study of signs is a study in the basic metaphysical questions that haunt humans everywhere: Why are we here? Who or what put us here? What, if anything, can be done about it? Who am I? and so on. The languages, myths, narratives, rituals, art works, and so forth to which human beings are exposed in specific cultural contexts guide their search to discover answers to these questions. Semiotics does not attempt to answer why these questions exist in the human species, because it knows that an answer is unlikely. Rather, it limits itself to a less grandiose project – describing the textual and representational activities they animate. Nevertheless, the semiotic agenda is starting to be shaped more and more by a search for the biological, psychic, and social roots of the human need for *meaning*, of the 'metaphysical story' behind the signs.

Semiotics is a dynamic, vibrant, ever-changing science. It is indeed remarkable that with barely a handful of notions and concepts, it can be used so insightfully to describe and understand such things as art, advertising, language, clothing, buildings, and, indeed, anything that is 'interesting' as a human product. Hopefully, the reader will have come away from this book with the singular verity – expressed so well by Charles Peirce – that as a species we are programmed to 'think only in signs.'

7.5 Further Reading and Online Resources

Further Reading

Barthes, Roland. *Système de la mode*. Paris: Seuil, 1967.
– *Mythologies*. Paris: Seuil, 1957.
Berger, Arthur A. *Manufacturing Desire: Media, Popular Culture, and Everyday Life*. New Brunswick, NJ: Transaction Publishers, 1996.
Goffman, Erving. *The Presentation of Self in Everyday Life*. Garden City, NY: Doubleday, 1959.
Gottdiener, M. *Postmodern Semiotics: Material Culture and the Forms of Postmodern Life*. London: Blackwell, 1995.
Levenstein, H. *Paradox of Plenty: A Social History of Eating in Modern America*. Oxford: Oxford University Press, 1993.
Lévi-Strauss, Claude. *Myth and Meaning: Cracking the Code of Culture*. Toronto: University of Toronto Press, 1978.
– *The Raw and the Cooked*. London: Jonathan Cape, 1964.
Mintz, S.W. *Tasting Food, Tasting Freedom: Excursions into Eating, Culture, and the Past*. Boston: Beacon, 1996.
Petrilli, Susan, and Augusto Ponzio. *Semiotics Unbounded: Interpretive Routes through the Open Network of Signs*. Toronto: University of Toronto Press, 2005.
Rubinstein, R.P. *Dress Codes: Meanings and Messages in American Culture*. Boulder, CO: Westview, 1995.
Schlosser, E. *Fast Food Nation*. Boston: Houghton Mifflin, 2000.
Steele, Valerie. *Fetish: Fashion, Sex, and Power*. Oxford: Oxford University Press, 1995.
Visser, M. *The Rituals of Dinner*. New York: HarperCollins, 1991.

Online Resources

For online links to work on the semiotics of food and clothing, the reader can consult the excellent site Tools for Cultural Studies (http://pages.unibas.ch/shine/culturalstudies.html#food).

Notes

1 What Is Semiotics?

1 Ferdinand de Saussure, *Cours de linguistique générale*, ed. C. Bally and A. Sechehaye (Paris: Payot, 1916); trans. W. Baskin, *Course in General Linguistics* (New York: McGraw-Hill, 1958), 15–16.
2 Ibid., 68.
3 Ibid., 112.
4 John Deely, *Four Ages of Understanding: The First Postmodern Survey of Philosophy from Ancient Times to the Turn of the Twentieth Century* (Toronto: University of Toronto Press, 2001).
5 C.K. Ogden and I.A. Richards, *The Meaning of Meaning* (New York: Harcourt, Brace and World, 1923).
6 C.E. Osgood, G.J. Suci, and P.H. Tannenbaum, *The Measurement of Meaning* (Urbana: University of Illinois Press, 1957).
7 Leonard Bloomfield, *Language* (New York: Holt, Rinehart, and Winston, 1933).
8 Umberto Eco, *Semiotics and the Philosophy of Language* (Bloomington: Indiana University Press, 1984), 46–86.
9 Umberto Eco, *A Theory of Semiotics* (Bloomington: Indiana University Press, 1976), 74.

2 Signs

1 Thomas A. Sebeok, *Signs: An Introduction to Semiotics* (Toronto: University of Toronto Press, 1994).
2 The pivotal work and ideas of Morris Swadesh in the 1950s led to the development of sound symbolism theory and especially the investigation

of its role in word origins. See, for example, his book *The Origins and Diversification of Language* (Chicago: Aldine-Atherton, 1971).

3 Charles S. Peirce, *Collected Papers*, ed. C. Hartshorne and P. Weiss (Cambridge: Harvard University Press, 1931–1958), 2:228.

4 Thomas A. Sebeok, *Essays in Zoosemiotics* (Toronto: Toronto Semiotic Circle, 1994).

5 Ray L. Birdwhistell, *Introduction to Kinesics* (Ann Arbor: University of Michigan, 1952).

6 Paul Ekman and Wallace Friesen, *Unmasking the Face* (Englewood Cliffs, NJ: Prentice-Hall, 1975).

7 Desmond Morris, *The Human Zoo* (London: Cape, 1969), 89.

8 Edward T. Hall, *The Hidden Dimension* (New York: Doubleday, 1966).

9 Desmond Morris et al., *Gestures: Their Origins and Distributions* (London: Cape, 1979).

10 David McNeill, *Hand and Mind: What Gestures Reveal about Thought* (Chicago: University of Chicago Press, 1992); and idem, *Gesture & Thought* (Chicago: University of Chicago Press, 2005).

11 Denise Schmandt-Besserat, 'The Earliest Precursor of Writing,' *Scientific American* 238 (1978): 50–9.

12 D. Ingram, 'Typology and Universals of Personal Pronouns,' in J.H. Greenberg, ed., *Universals of Human Language* (Stanford: Stanford University Press, 1978), 213–47.

13 W.H. Thorpe, *Bird-Song* (Cambridge: Cambridge University Press, 1961).

3 Structure

1 Henry Miller, *Sexus* (New York: Grove, 1949), 231.

2 Claude Lévi-Strauss, *Structural Anthropology* (New York: Basic, 1958).

3 George Lakoff and Mark Johnson, *Metaphors We Live By* (Chicago: University of Chicago Press, 1980).

4 'Have Only Men Evolved?' in Ruth Hubbard, Mary Sue Henifin, and Barbara Fried, eds., *Biological Woman: The Convenient Myth* (Cambridge, MA: Shenkman, 1983), 34.

5 I.A. Richards, *The Philosophy of Rhetoric* (Oxford: Oxford University Press, 1936).

6 Solomon Asch, 'On the Use of Metaphor in the Description of Persons,' in H. Werner, ed., *On Expressive Language* (Worcester: Clark University Press, 1955), 86–94.

7 M. Emantian, 'Metaphor and the Expression of Emotion: The Value of Cross-Cultural Perspectives,' *Metaphor and Symbolic Activity* 10 (1995): 163–82.

8   A collection of studies examining the contribution of Zipf to the study of change in language and communication generally can be found in the journal *Glottometrics* 4 (2002). In that issue four studies are worthy of mention here: V.K. Balasubrahmanyan and S. Naranan ('Algorithmic Information, Complexity and Zipf's Law,' 1–26) argue that frequency distribution is not insensitive to meaning, as many Zipfian analysts claim. Thorsten Roelcke ('Efficiency of Communication: A New Concept of Language Economy,' 27–38) stresses that before Zipf, the phenomenon of linguistic economy was hardly known, thus constituting a veritable scientific discovery. Eric S. Wheeler ('Zipf's Law and Why It Works Everywhere,' 45–8) criticizes how Zipf's Law has been abused and applied to prove virtually anything one wants to. Marcelo A. Montemurro and D. Zanette ('Frequency-Rank Distribution of Words in Large Text Samples: Phenomenology and Models,' 87–98) supports the original formulas that Zipf posited because they seem to work consistently with large text samples.

9   Edward R. Tufte, *The Cognitive Style of PowerPoint* (New York: Graphics Press, 2003).

10   Václav Havel, *Disturbing the Peace* (New York: Vintage, 1990), 59.

11   George Eliot, *Daniel Deronda* (Oxford: Clarendon, 1980), 89.

12   Roland Barthes, *Mythologies* (Paris: Seuil, 1957).

13   Roland Barthes, *Elements of Semiology* (London: Jonathan Cape, 1967), 47.

4 Codes

1   Cited in Paul Perron and Marcel Danesi, eds., *Classic Readings in Semiotics* (Ottawa: Legas Press, 2003), 34.

2   Ibid., 42.

3   Ibid., 43.

4   Ibid., 43.

5   Ibid., 44.

6   Ferdinand de Saussure, *Cours de linguistique générale*, ed. C. Bally and A. Sechehaye (Paris: Payot, 1916); trans. W. Baskin, *Course in General Linguistics* (New York: McGraw-Hill, 1958), 6.

7   Edward T. Hall, *The Hidden Dimension* (New York: Doubleday, 1966); idem, *The Silent Language* (New York: Anchor, 1973).

8   Vladimir Propp, *Morphology of the Folktale* (Austin: University of Texas Press, 1928).

9   Ibid.

10   Lucien Tesnière, *Éléments de syntaxe structurale* (Paris: Klincksieck, 1958), 102.

11 Robert Levine, *A Geography of Time: The Temporal Misadventures of a Social Psychologist or How Every Culture Keeps Time Just a Little Bit Differently* (New York: Basic, 1997).

5 Texts

1 Susanne Langer, *Philosophy in a New Key* (Cambridge, MA: Harvard University Press, 1948).
2 Work on cross-species semiosis is a growing subfield in semiotics. It is known as *biosemiotics*, as already discussed (§1.5, §2.3). Information on its overall objectives and methodology (including facts about interesting animal communication phenomena such as the honeybee dance) can be found in Thomas A. Sebeok and Marcel Danesi, *The Forms of Meaning: Modeling Systems Theory and Semiotics* (Berlin: Mouton de Gruyter, 2000).
3 Julia Kristeva, *Séméiotiké: Recherches pour un sémanalyse* (Paris: Seuil, 1969).
4 Roland Barthes, 'Theory of the Text,' in Robert Young, ed., *Untying the Text* (London: Routledge, 1981), 31–47.
5 Todorov's proposal is found in his book *Theories of the Symbol* (Ithaca, NY: Cornell University Press, 1982).
6 Rudolf Arnheim, *Visual Thinking* (Berkeley: University of California Press, 1969); John Berger, *Ways of Seeing* (Harmondsworth: Penguin, 1972).
7 Clifford Geertz, *The Interpretation of Cultures* (New York: Harper Torch, 1973), 23.

6 Representation

1 Thomas Kuhn, *The Structure of Scientific Revolutions* (Chicago: University of Chicago Press, 1970).
2 Marshall McLuhan, *The Gutenberg Galaxy* (Toronto: University of Toronto Press, 1962).
3 Roland Barthes, *Mythologies* (Paris: Seuil, 1957).
4 Ibid.
5 Umberto Eco, *Serendipities: Language and Lunacy*, trans. William Weaver (New York: Columbia University Press, 1998).
6 R.K. Merton and E. Barber, *The Travels and Adventures of Serendipity: A Study in Sociological Semantics and the Sociology of Science* (Princeton, NJ: Princeton University Press, 2003).
7 Ian Stewart, foreword to I. Moscovich, *1000 PlayThinks* (New York: Workman Publishing, 2001), v.

7 Applications

1 L.S. Dubin, *The History of Beads* (New York: Abrams, 1987), 134.
2 Roland Barthes, *Système de la mode* (Paris: Seuil, 1967).
3 Claude Lévi-Strauss, *The Raw and the Cooked* (London: Jonathan Cape, 1964).
4 Susan Sontag, *Illness as Metaphor* (New York: Farrar, Straus and Giroux, 1978), 7.
5 Jacalyn Duffin, *Disease Concepts in History* (Toronto: University of Toronto Press, 2005).

Glossary of Technical Terms

This glossary contains most of the technical terms introduced in this book. It also has others that are used in semiotics. It is thus a kind of 'working dictionary' of semiotic terms.

Abstract concept   A concept that cannot be demonstrated or observed directly; it can only be imagined.

Actant   A unit of narration (a hero, an opponent) that surfaces in all kinds of stories.

Addressee   The receiver of a message.

Addresser   The sender of a message.

Aesthesia   The experience of sensation; in art, it refers to the fact that the senses and feelings are stimulated holistically by art texts.

Aesthetics   The study of the meaning and interpretation of art in general.

Alliteration   The repetition of the initial consonant sounds or sound clusters of words.

Alphabet   The graphic code whereby individual characters stand for specific sounds (or sound combinations).

Analogy   The structural relation whereby a form replaces another that is similar in structure, function, or use.

Archetype	The term coined by psychoanalyst Carl Jung to designate any unconscious image that manifests itself in dreams, myths, art forms, and performances across cultures.
Architext	The prototype from which other or subsequent texts are derived.
Artefact	An object produced or shaped by human craft, especially a tool, a weapon, or an ornament that is of archaeological or historical interest.
Axiom	A statement universally accepted as true and therefore accepted without proof.
Basic-level concept	The concept that has a typological (classificatory) function.
Biosemiotics	The branch of semiotics that studies semiosis in all life forms.
Biosphere	The physical environment to which an organism adapts.
Channel	The physical means by which a signal or message is transmitted.
Character	The person portrayed in an artistic piece, such as a drama or novel.
Closed text	The text that elicits a singular, or a very limited, range of interpretations.
Clothing	Apparel to cover the body.
Code	The system in which signs are organized and that determines how they relate to one another and can thus be used for representation and communication.
Communication	Social interaction through message exchange; the production and exchange of messages and meanings; the use of specific modes and media to transmit messages.

Conative function	The effect of a message on the addressee.
Concept	A general thought connection or pattern encoded by as sign or signs (within cultural contexts).
Conceptual metaphor	A generalized metaphorical formula that undergirds a specific abstraction.
Conceptual metonym	A generalized metonymical formula that undergirds a specific abstraction.
Concrete concept	A concept that is demonstrable and observable in a direct way.
Connotation	The extended or secondary meaning of a sign; the symbolic or mythic meaning of a certain signifier (word, image, etc.).
Contact	The physical channel employed in communication and the psychological connections made between addresser and addressee.
Context	The environment (physical and social) in which signs are produced and messages interpreted.
Conventional sign	A sign that is made by human ingenuity .
Culture	The interconnected system of meanings encoded by signs and texts.
Decoding	The process of deciphering the message formed in terms of a specific code.
Deconstruction	The view that texts can be deconstructed into a series of differences (oppositions) and, thus, that they do not refer to anything outside of themselves in any 'true' fashion.
Denotation	The primary, intentional meaning of a sign.
Diachrony	The study of changes in signs and codes over time.
Discourse	Verbal communication involving an addresser and an addressee.

Distance	The space that people maintain between themselves during socially meaningful contact or interaction.
Dress	A meaningful system of clothing (e.g., the dress code for weddings).
Emotive function	The addresser's emotional intent in communicating something.
Encoding	The process of putting together a message in terms of a specific code.
Entropy	Anything that is unpredictable in a message.
Feedback	Information, signals, cues issuing from the receiver of a message as detected by the sender, allowing him or her to adjust the message in order to make it clearer, more meaningful, more effective.
Fiction	A literary work whose content is produced by the imagination; not necessarily based on fact.
Firstness	In Peircean theory, the first level of meaning derived from bodily and sensory processes.
Gender	Sexual identity established in cultural terms.
Gesticulant	The gesture unit accompanying speech.
Gesticulation	The use of gestures to accompany speech.
Gesture	Semiosis and representation by means of the hands, the arms, and to a lesser extent the head.
Ground	The meaning of a metaphor.
Haptics	The study of touching patterns during social interaction.
Hermeneutics	The study and interpretation of texts.
Hieroglyphic writing	Ancient Egyptian system of writing, in which pictorial symbols were used to represent meanings or sounds or a combination of meanings and sound.

Homonymy	Two or more words that are spelled or pronounced the same but have different meanings.
Hypertext	A text within another text explaining some component of the other text.
Hypertextuality	A system for linking different texts and images within a computer document or over a network.
Hypoicon	Peirce's term for an icon that is shaped by cultural convention but that nonetheless can be figured out by those who are not members of the culture.
Hypotext	A text based on another text, which, however, it alters, elaborates, or extends.
Icon	A sign in which the signifier has a direct (nonarbitrary), simulative connection to its signified or referent.
Iconicity	The process of representing something with iconic signs.
Image schema	The term used by George Lakoff and Mark Johnson to refer to the recurring structures of, or in, our perceptual interactions, bodily experiences, and cognitive operations that portray locations, movements, shapes, and so on in the mind.
Index	A sign in which the signifier has an existential connection to its signified or referent (i.e., the sign indicates that something 'exists' somewhere in time or space).
Indexicality	The process of representing something with indexical signs.
Information	Any fact or datum that can be stored and retrieved by humans or machines.
Interpretant	The process of adapting a sign's meaning to personal and social experiences.

Interpretation	The process of deciphering what a sign or text means.
Intertext	A text to which another text refers.
Intertextuality	The allusion within a text to some other text of which the interpreter would normally have knowledge.
Irony	The use of words to express something different from and often opposite to their literal meaning; the use of words in a humorous but often sarcastic way.
Kinesics	The study of bodily semiosis.
Legisign	In Peircean theory, a representamen (signifier) that designates something by convention.
Logograph	A full symbol or character representing a word.
Logographic writing	A semisymbolic writing system in which a character, known as a logograph, resembles its referent only in small part.
Map	A visual text representing a culturally significant territory or space drawn with a combination of iconic, indexical, and symbolic techniques.
Meaning	A concept that is understandable in personal and cultural ways.
Medium	The technical or physical means by which a message is transmitted.
Message	The meaning of a text.
Metalingual function	A communicative function by which the code being used is identified.
Metaphor	A semiotic process by which two referential domains (A, B) are connected (A is B).
Metatext	A text that makes an explicit or implicit critical commentary on another text.

Metonymy	A semiotic process by which an entity is used to refer to another that is related to it.
Myth	A story that aims to explain the origin of life or of the universe in terms of some metaphysical or deistic entity or entities.
Mythology	The use and/or evocation of mythic themes in contemporary behaviours and performances; the study of myths.
Name	A sign that identifies a person or place.
Narrative structure	A universal pattern of storytelling based on a series of oppositions (hero vs opponent) that generate plot, character, setting, and so on.
Narrative	Something told or written, such as an account, story, or tale.
Narratology	The branch of semiotics that studies narrativity.
Narrator	The teller of the narrative.
Natural medium	Any biologically inherited ability or capacity for encoding and decoding a message, including the voice (speech), the face (expressions), and the body (gesture, posture, etc.).
Natural sign	A sign produced by nature (such as a symptom).
Natural transmission	The transmission of messages naturally (through the air channel, through chemical signals, etc.).
Noise	Anything that interferes with the reception of a message.
Novel	A fictional prose narrative in which characters and situations are depicted within the framework of a plot.
Object	What a sign refers to.
Onomastics	The study of names.

Onomatopoeia	A verbal representation through the simulation of one or several of the sonorous properties of referents.
Ontogenesis	The development of all semiosic abilities during childhood.
Open text	A text that entails a complex interpretive range.
Opposition	The process by which signs are differentiated through a minimal change in their form or meaning.
Paradigmatic	A structural relation between signs that keeps them distinct and therefore recognizable.
Paratext	The physical and conventional characteristics associated with certain kinds of texts, such as their physical structure, titles, headings, prefaces, epigraphs, dedications, acknowledgments, footnotes, illustrations, and dust jackets.
Performance	Representation and communication of some text, framed in a special way and put on display for an audience.
Perspective	The technique of representing three-dimensional objects and depth relationships on a two-dimensional surface.
Phatic function	A communicative function by which contact between addresser and addressee is established.
Phoneme	A minimal unit of sound in a language that allows its users to differentiate meanings.
Phylogenesis	The evolution of all semiosic abilities in the human species.
Pictographic writing	A type of writing system in which a sign, known as a pictograph, bears pictorial resemblance to its referent.

Plot	The plan of events or main story in a narrative or drama.
Poetic function	A communicative function based on poetic language.
Poetry	Verbal art based on the acoustic, rhythmic, and imagistic properties of words.
Pop art	An art form that utilizes themes and images taken from mass technological culture.
Postmodernism	The world view that all knowledge is relative and human-made, and that there is no purpose to life beyond the immediate and the present.
Post-structuralism	A movement in semiotics countering the structuralist notion that signs encode some aspect of reality.
Proxemics	A branch of semiotics and anthropology that studies the symbolic structure of the physical space maintained between people.
Qualisign	In Peircean theory, the representamen (signifier) that refers to a quality.
Receiver	The person to whom a message or text is directed.
Redundancy	That which is predictable or conventional in a message or text, thus helping counteract the potential interference effects of noise.
Referent	What is referred to (any object, being, idea, or event).
Referential domain	The specific range of meanings to which a sign or text refers.
Referential function	A communicative act in which there is a straightforward connection between the act and what it refers to.
Representamen	In Peircean theory, the physical part of a sign.

Representation	The process by which referents are captured and organized in some way by signs or texts.
Secondness	In Peircean theory, the second level of meaning derived from relating signs to one another or to other elements (including sign makers and sign users).
Semantic differential	A technique used in semiotics for fleshing our connotations.
Semiology	Saussure's term for the study of signs.
Semiosis	The comprehension and production of signs.
Semiosphere	The world of signs, codes, and texts to be differentiated from the biosphere (the physical, life-supporting environment).
Semiotics	The science that studies signs and their uses in representation.
Sender	The transmitter of a message or text.
Setting	The place and conditions in which a narrative takes place.
Sign language	The language code based on gestures and grammatical rules that share common elements with spoken language.
Sign	Something that stands for something or someone else in some capacity.
Signal	An emission or movement that naturally or conventionally triggers some reaction on the part of a receiver.
Signification	The process of generating meaning through the use of signs.
Signified	That part of a sign which is referred to.
Signifier	That part of a sign that does the referring; the physical part of a sign.
Sinsign	In Peircean theory, a representamen (signifier) that draws attention to or singles out a particular object in time-space.

Sound symbolism	The process by which referents are represented through some form of vocal simulation.
Source domain	The class of vehicles that deliver a conceptual metaphor.
Structuralism	The study of the structures (signs, texts, codes) generated by semiosis.
Structure	Any repeatable, systematic, patterned, or predictable aspect of signs, codes, and texts.
Subordinate level	The level at which a concept has a detailing function.
Subtext	The text (message) hidden within a text.
Superordinate level	The level at which a concept has a highly general classificatory function.
Syllable	The word or part of a word pronounced with a single, uninterrupted sounding of the voice (usually a vowel) and generally one or more sounds of lesser sonority (usually consonants).
Symbol	A sign that represents a referent through cultural convention.
Symbolism	The process of representing something with symbols.
Symptom	A bodily sign that stands for some ailment, physical condition, or disease.
Synchronic	The study of signs at a specific point in time (usually the present).
Synesthesia	The juxtaposition of signs so as to evoke different sense modalities simultaneously.
Synonymy	The relation by which the meanings of different signs overlap.
Syntagmatic	A structural relation that guides the combination of signs or parts of signs in a coherent and consistent way.

Target domain	The topic of a conceptual metaphor.
Text	A 'larger sign' put together in terms of a specific code.
Textuality	The process of generating and utilizing texts for representational purposes.
Thirdness	In Peircean theory, the third level of meaning derived from symbolic processes.
Topic	The subject of a metaphor (tenor).
Transmission	The physical process of sending messages or texts to a receiver.
Trope	A figure of speech.
Vehicle	The part of a metaphor to which a topic is connected.
Whorfian hypothesis	The view elaborated by Benjamin Lee Whorf that the language one speaks shapes one's world view.
Writing	The process of representing speech with characters.
Zoosemiosis	Semiosis in animal species.
Zoosemiotics	The branch of semiotics studying semiosis in animals.

Index